ADAM HAMILTON

CHRISTIANITY'S FAMILY TREE

WHAT OTHER CHRISTIANS BELIEVE AND WHY

D1277282

LEADER'S GUIDE
by Sally D. Sharpe

ABINGDON PRESS
Nashville

Christianity's Family Tree
What Other Christians Believe and Why

Leader's Guide

Copyright © 2007 by Abingdon Press.

Scripture quotations in this publication, unless otherwise indicated, are from the New Revised Standard Version of the Bible, copyrighted © 1989 by the Division of Christian Education of the National Council of the Churches of Christ in the United States of America, and are used by permission.

This book is printed on acid-free, elemental chlorine-free paper.

ISBN 978-0-687-46671-9

07 08 09 10 11 12 13 14 15 16—10 9 8 7 6 5 4 3 2 1

MANUFACTURED IN THE UNITED STATES OF AMERICA

CONTENTS

HOW TO USE THIS LEADER'S GUIDE

When it comes to the Christian family tree, most of us know very little about the beliefs and practices of our "relatives" on branches of the tree other than our own. If we were to attend a family reunion of our Christian brothers and sisters from every denomination, most of us would be inclined to sit and talk with those we attend church with week after week, rather than to venture out of our comfort zone and get to know those who are different from us. Yet the truth is, we all are connected to one another. We are family. And as we learn about one another, we learn something about ourselves.

Participating in this study will be somewhat like attending a family reunion. For the next eight weeks, we will be getting to know our family in the faith. Specifically, we will explore eight different denominations or traditions of the Christian faith, seeing what makes each branch of our Christian family unique. The aim of the study is not to critique the various churches and traditions; neither is it to compare and contrast them. Rather, its purpose is threefold:

1. to help us gain an appreciation for the richness of the various Christian traditions;
2. to give us a better understanding of church history;
3. to enrich our own faith experience by exploring the faith and practices of our brothers and sisters in the Christian family.

Christianity's Family Tree may be used as a stand-alone study by Sunday school classes and other small groups meeting at other times during the week or as part of a congregational emphasis and outreach event on the rich diversity of the Christian family—a topic appealing to people both inside and outside the church. A separate Pastor's Guide with CD-ROM provides all the information and tools needed to take this study beyond the classroom, beyond the sanctuary, and into the community, bringing people into the church who otherwise might attend only at Christmas or Easter. Included are helpful materials such as suggestions for gathering support, designing a kick-off event, and planning worship services; promotional ideas and materials, including postcards, posters, and flyers; actual sermon starters, illustrations, and video clips; and more.

Whether you will be leading a stand-alone study or joining other small groups in a congregational emphasis and outreach event, you will want to make group members aware of the accompanying participant's book which expands on the weekly video presentations. Participants may choose to read the corresponding chapter either before or after the weekly group session. Although the book is not a required resource, it will greatly enhance the study experience and serve as a helpful resource to have on hand. Ideally, participants should have the opportunity to purchase copies of the book prior to your first group session. If this is not possible, introduce them to the book during your first group session and try to obtain copies prior to your second session.

A Quick Overview

As group leader, your role will be to facilitate the weekly sessions using this Leader's Guide and the accompanying DVD. Because no two groups are alike, this guide has been designed to give you flexibility and choice in tailoring the sessions for your group. You may choose one of the following format options, *or you may adapt these as you wish to meet the schedule and needs of your particular group.* (Note: The times indicated within parentheses are merely estimates.

6

You may move at a faster or slower pace, making adjustments as necessary to fit your schedule.)

Basic Option: 60 minutes

Opening Prayer . . . . (2 minutes)
Biblical Foundation . . . . (3 minutes)
Video Presentation . . . . (15 minutes)
Group Discussion . . . . (30 minutes)
Taking It Home . . . . (5 minutes)
Closing Prayer . . . . (< 5 minutes)

Extended Option: 90 minutes

Opening Prayer . . . . (2 minutes)
Biblical Foundation . . . . (3 minutes)
Opening Activity . . . . (10–15 minutes)
Video Presentation . . . . (15 minutes)
Group Discussion . . . . (30 minutes)
Group Activity . . . . (15 minutes)
Taking It Home . . . . (5 minutes)
Closing Prayer . . . . (< 5 minutes)

Although you are encouraged to adapt the sessions to meet your needs, you also are encouraged to make Scripture and prayer regular components of the weekly group sessions. The Scripture verses provided for each session are intended to serve as a biblical foundation for the group session as well as for participants' continuing reflection and application during the following week. Similarly, the opening and closing prayers are offered so that you may "cover" the group session in prayer. The opening prayer invites God to prepare participants' hearts and minds so that they might learn from another faith tradition and thus enrich their own faith. The closing prayer asks God to help participants apply the biblical principles and practical insights they have gained. (Feel free to use these printed prayers, or create your own.)

In addition to the components outlined in the suggested format options, the following "leader helps" are provided to equip you for each group session:

Main Idea . . . . (session theme)

Session Goals . . . . (objectives for the group session)

Key Insights . . . . (summary of main points from the video)

Leader Extra . . . . (additional information related to topic)

Notable Quote . . . . (noteworthy quote from the video)

You may use these helps for your personal preparation only, or you may choose to incorporate them into the group session in some way. For example, you might choose to write the Main Idea and/or Session Goals on a chalkboard or large sheet of paper prior to the beginning of class, review the Key Insights from the video either before or after group discussion, incorporate the Leader Extra into group discussion, or close with the Notable Quote.

At the end of the materials provided for each group session, you will find a reproducible Participant Handout. This handout includes an abbreviated summary of the Key Insights from the video and Taking It Home application exercises for the coming week. Each week you will have the opportunity to remind participants that these exercises are designed to help them get the most out of this study that they possibly can. They alone are the ones who will determine whether this is just another group study or a transformational experience that will have a lasting, positive impact on their lives.

Helpful Hints

Here are a few helpful hints for preparing and leading the weekly group sessions:

- Become familiar with the material before the group session. If possible, watch the video segment in advance.
- Choose the various components you will use during the group session, including the specific discussion questions you plan to cover. (Highlight these or put a checkmark beside them. Remember, you do not have to use all the questions provided; and you even can create your own.)
- Secure a TV and DVD player in advance; oversee room setup.
- Begin and end on time.
- Be enthusiastic. Remember, you set the tone for the class.
- Create a climate of participation, encouraging individuals to participate as they feel comfortable.
- Communicate the importance of group discussions and group exercises.
- To stimulate group discussion, consider reviewing the Key Insights first and then asking participants to tell what they saw as the highlights of the video.
- If no one answers at first, do not be afraid of a little silence. Count to seven silently; then say something, such as, "Would anyone like to go first?" If no one responds, venture an answer yourself. Then ask for comments and other responses.
- Model openness as you share with the group. Group members will follow your example. If you share at a surface level, everyone else will follow suit.
- Draw out participants without asking them to share what they are unwilling to share. Make eye contact with someone and say something, such as, "How about someone else?"
- Encourage multiple answers or responses before moving on.
- Ask "Why?" or "Why do you believe that?" to help continue a discussion and give it greater depth.
- Affirm others' responses with positive comments, such as, "Great" or "Thanks" or "Good insight"—especially if this is the first time someone has spoken during the group session.

- Give everyone a chance to talk, but keep the conversation moving. Moderate to prevent a few individuals from doing all the talking.
- Monitor your own contributions. If you are doing most of the talking, back off so that you do not train the group not to respond.
- Remember that you do not have to have all the answers. Your job is to keep the discussion going and encourage participation.
- Honor the time schedule. If a session is running longer than expected, get consensus from the group before continuing beyond the agreed-upon ending time.
- Consider involving group members in various aspects of the group session, such as asking for volunteers to play the DVD, read the prayers or say their own, read the Scripture, and so forth.

Above all, remember to pray. Pray for God to prepare and guide you, pray for your group members by name and for what God may do in their lives, and pray for God's presence and leading before each group session. Prayer will both encourage and empower you for the weeks ahead.

Finally, if you are a first-time leader, remember that many characters in the Bible were hesitant and unsure of accepting God's call to lead; but God never abandoned any of them. Rest assured that God will be with you, too. After all, Jesus promised, "I am with you always, to the end of the age" (Matthew 28:20).

ORTHODOXY: MYSTERY, LITURGY, AND TRADITION

Main Idea: *Orthodox worship shows us the importance of gathering with other Christians to remember that we are participants in a divine reality greater than this world.*

Getting Started

Session Goals

This session is intended to help participants . . .

- become familiar with some of the beliefs and practices of the Orthodox church;
- realize why Orthodoxy claims to be the "oldest child" of the Christian family and the one true church;
- understand the symbolic significance of the Orthodox worship environment and experience.

Opening Prayer

Dear God, we come together today to learn about one of the branches of the Christian family tree, Orthodoxy. We ask you to remind us that our aim is not to critique the Orthodox faith tradition but to learn from it so that our own faith might be enriched. Help us through our study and discussion to become more authentic and effective disciples of your Son, Jesus Christ. We affirm that all who call upon his

11

name are members of one body, one faith. May we be united in spirit, in love, and in service so that your kingdom work may be accomplished in our world. In Jesus' name we pray. Amen.

Biblical Foundation

Now faith is the assurance of things hoped for, the conviction of things not seen. Indeed, by faith our ancestors received approval. By faith we understand that the worlds were prepared by the word of God, so that what is seen was made from things that are not visible. . . .

By faith Abraham obeyed when he was called to set out for a place that he was to receive as an inheritance; and he set out, not knowing where he was going. By faith he stayed for a time in the land he had been promised, as in a foreign land, living in tents, as did Isaac and Jacob, who were heirs with him of the same promise. For he looked forward to the city that has foundations, whose architect and builder is God. . . .

All of these died in faith without having received the promises, but from a distance they saw and greeted them. They confessed that they were strangers and foreigners on the earth, for people who speak in this way make it clear that they are seeking a homeland. If they had been thinking of the land that they had left behind, they would have had opportunity to return. But as it is, they desire a better country, that is, a heavenly one. Therefore God is not ashamed to be called their God; indeed, he has prepared a city for them.

Therefore, since we are surrounded by so great a cloud of witnesses, let us also lay aside every weight and the sin that clings so closely, and let us run with perseverance the race that is set before us, looking to Jesus the pioneer and perfecter of our faith, who for the sake of the joy that was set before him endured the cross, disregarding its shame, and has taken his seat at the right hand of the throne of God. (Hebrews 11:1-3, 8-10, 13-16; 12:1-2)

Leader Extra

The Nicene Creed

The beliefs of the Orthodox church are summarized in the Nicene Creed, which is recited at each celebration of the liturgy:

We believe in one God, the Father, the Almighty, maker of heaven and earth, of all that is, seen and unseen.

We believe in one Lord, Jesus Christ, the only Son of God, eternally begotten of the Father, God from God, Light from Light, true God from true God, begotten, not made, of one Being with the Father, through him all things were made. For us and for our salvation he came down from heaven; by the power of the Holy Spirit he became incarnate from the Virgin Mary, and became truly human. For our sake he was crucified under Pontius Pilate; he suffered death and was buried.

On the third day he rose again in accordance with the Scriptures; he ascended into heaven and is seated at the right hand of the Father. He will come again in glory to judge the living and the dead, and his kingdom will have no end.

We believe in the Holy Spirit, the Lord, the giver of life, who proceeds from the Father. Who with the Father and the Son is worshiped and glorified, who has spoken through the Prophets. We believe in one holy catholic and apostolic Church. We acknowledge one baptism for the forgiveness of sins. We look for the resurrection of the dead, and the life of the world to come. Amen.[1]

In the seventh century, at a regional council in Toledo, Spain, Western Christians added three words to the Nicene Creed without consulting Eastern Christians. These three words, called the "filioque" (Latin for "from the Son"), stated that the Holy Spirit proceeds not only from the Father, which everyone agreed upon, but also from the Son. Disagreement over this phrase, in addition to conflicts over papal authority and liturgy, led to a breach between the Eastern and Western Christians in 1054, which has lasted to this day.

Today the Nicene Creed is still the prince of creeds among Christians, with Roman Catholics and mainline Protestants including the "filioque" in their versions of the creed. With this one exception, the majority of Christians are in agreement when it comes to the essentials of the faith affirmed in the Nicene Creed.

Opening Activity

Write the Nicene Creed on a chalkboard or large sheet of paper. (You may want to do this before class starts.) Read the creed in unison and then discuss the following:

• Would you agree that the Nicene Creed summarizes the essentials of the Christian faith?
• What are the three basic or primary affirmations of the creed?
• How is the creed similar to/different from affirmations of faith recited in your church? (Point out the addition of the phrase "and the Son," the "filioque," in the Nicene Creed used by Roman Catholics and Protestants.)

Learning Together

Video Presentation

Play the video segment for Week 1, *Orthodoxy.*
Running Time: 17:58 minutes

Key Insights

1. We are connected to all Christians, regardless of denomination, by our belief in the same Father, the same Lord (Jesus Christ), and the same Holy Spirit. As we learn from one another, we come to understand our own stories better and be more-faithful disciples of Jesus Christ.
2. Orthodoxy claims to be the tradition that holds most closely to the traditions of the early church. *Orthodox* means "right

worship" and "right doctrine." The official stance of the Orthodox church is that they are the one true church.

3. The Orthodox church bases its doctrine on Christ, the Scriptures (both Old and New Testaments), and the ecumenical councils that summarized the beliefs of the early church (such as the Nicene Creed).

4. Orthodox Christians place an emphasis on both Scripture and tradition. They consider the early church Fathers as interpreters of the Bible whose writings bear witness to what it means to be a Christian.

5. Orthodox worship is a mystical experience designed to help worshipers "see" divine reality.
   • The dome in many Orthodox churches signifies the cosmos and reminds worshipers of the vastness of God's kingdom and God's presence, which continually surround us.
   • Icons of saints and martyrs remind worshipers that they are also surrounded by a great cloud of witnesses.
   • Each service includes the liturgy of the Word (reading from the Holy Scriptures) and the liturgy of the Eucharist, which includes remembering the cross, the tomb, the Resurrection, the Ascension, and the Second Coming—something yet to happen in earthly terms but already accomplished in mystical terms.

6. Orthodox worship shows us the importance of gathering with other Christians to remember that this is not the real world and that we are surrounded by a great cloud of witnesses, which builds our faith.

Leader Extra
Orthodox Beliefs and Practices
• *The Human Condition*—The Orthodox do not teach the doctrine of original sin. They do not believe that Adam and Eve's sin is now passed on to all humankind. What is passed on from Adam and Eve is death and all that death brings: anger, lust, hate, greed, fear, sickness. As a result, humanity was placed in the grip of death

and the devil. Jesus came to redeem humankind from death and the devil by giving his own life.

- *Sacraments*—Like Roman Catholics, the Orthodox recognize seven official sacraments, while maintaining that a host of things may function as sacraments (means of God's grace coming into our lives). The Orthodox believe that each of the sacraments is used by the Holy Spirit to impart grace and make us holy.

- *Baptism*—The Christian life begins at baptism; and until one is baptized, one is outside the church. Baptism in Orthodox churches is by immersion, and even infants are immersed completely under the water. Anointing with oil (chrismation) follows immediately after baptism. This takes the place of confirmation, so that one is fully a member of the church at baptism. Among the first acts after baptism is the reception of the Eucharist; a drop of wine is placed on the tongue of the infant.

- *Ordination of Priests*—Orthodox priests are men; women are not ordained in the Orthodox church. Unlike the Roman Catholic Church, priests may marry, provided they have married before ordination.

- *Scripture and Tradition*—The Orthodox believe that the Holy Spirit was guiding the early church and that, therefore, the Christians of the first five centuries were important interpreters of the Scriptures. The writings of these Christians function for the Orthodox in some ways like the Mishnah and the Talmud (scriptural interpretations and commentaries) function in Judaism. The Protestant idea of *sola scriptura* (Scripture alone) is unheard of in the Orthodox tradition. Scripture is the primary basis of authority in the faith, but it must be interpreted with the help of the Holy Spirit and the wisdom of the church through the ages as collected in many of its writings. This material includes stories of martyrs, letters, sermons, and other writings from the early church—beginning in AD 96 with the First Letter of Clement and stretching for hundreds of years.

16

Group Discussion

Note: More questions are provided than you may have time for. Select those you would like your group to discuss.

1. How are we connected to all Christians, regardless of denomination? What might we learn from one another, and how might this benefit us?

2. What claim does the Orthodox church make, and what is the basis for this claim? What does *orthodox* mean? What insights does this definition give you into the philosophy of the Orthodox church?

3. On what does the Orthodox church base its doctrine? What is the significance of the Nicene Creed to the Orthodox church?

4. *If you did the Opening Activity:* How does the Nicene Creed of the Orthodox church differ from that used by Roman Catholics and Protestants, and what is the reason for this difference? How might the controversy surrounding the creed, and the breach that resulted between Eastern and Western Christians, be compared to some contemporary conflicts among Christians?

5. How does the Orthodox emphasis on Scripture and tradition differ from the *sola scriptura,* or "Scripture alone," principle that largely defined the Protestant Reformation? What role do the writings of the early church play in shaping Orthodox doctrine and practice? (See Leader Extra: Orthodox Beliefs and Practices.)

6. What is Orthodox worship designed to help worshipers remember? How do both the worship environment and the worship experience help to achieve this? How might your own church be more effective in helping you to "see" divine reality? (Consider various environments and experiences.)

7. In addition to the great saints of the faith, who are the saints in the cloud of witnesses surrounding you? Name some of them and tell how they have helped to encourage you in your faith journey.

8. What have you learned from our study of the Orthodox church that will help to deepen your own faith and experience of God?

Group Activity

Divide the participants into small groups and have each group discuss the following: How would you live differently if you knew *absolutely and without question* that God is constantly by your side? How would you look at such conditions as illness, pain, sorrow, and tragedy if you had actually seen heaven and knew it was more real than anything you see on this earth? How would you react to temptation if you believed without question that Jesus watches over you; that this life is only temporary; and that the saints stand around you, cheering you on?

Come back together and discuss as a full group: When we are sick or discouraged or feeling alone, how should our faith sustain us? How can we cultivate this kind of sustaining faith?

Wrapping Up

Taking It Home

Explain that there are two resources available to help participants with personal application each week.

First, there is the Participant Handout. Briefly review the Taking It Home application exercises included on the handout. Encourage participants to complete the activities during the coming week, reassuring them that they will not be asked to share any details with the group. The exercises are intended for their private use and are designed to help them get the most out of this study that they possibly can. They alone are the ones who will determine whether this is just another group study or a transformational experience that will have a lasting, positive impact on their lives.

Second, there is the accompanying participant's book, which expands on the material covered in the weekly video presentations. Invite those participants who have already purchased copies of the book to read the first chapter this week as a follow-up to this group session. (Note: Acknowledge that some participants may choose to read the corresponding chapters in advance of the group sessions week to week, which also is acceptable. It is a matter of personal preference.) Those participants who have not ordered/purchased copies of the book may want to do so now. Although the book is not a required resource, it will greatly enhance the study experience and serve as a helpful resource to have on hand.

Notable Quote

"There are so many things in the world . . . that challenge your faith and draw you away from God. And you . . . start thinking this little world is all there is. . . . The Orthodox [church] reminds us of the importance of gathering to remember the real world. And that produces faith."

—Adam Hamilton

Closing Prayer

Dear God, we are grateful for the witness of the Orthodox church, which reminds us that this world is only temporary. It seems so permanent to us, yet in our hearts we know there is a heavenly city; and we yearn for it. Help us to renew our commitment to gather together, remembering that we are surrounded by a great cloud of witnesses. May we cast aside the sin that easily entangles and run with perseverance the race that is set before us. In Jesus' name we pray. Amen.

1. Adapted from The Nicene Creed, in *The United Methodist Hymnal* (Copyright © 1989 by The United Methodist Publishing House); 880.

Week 1: Orthodoxy
Participant Handout

Therefore, since we are surrounded by so great a cloud of witnesses, let us also lay aside every weight and the sin that clings so closely, and let us run with perseverance the race that is set before us, looking to Jesus the pioneer and perfecter of our faith.

(Hebrews 12:1-2)

Key Insights

1. We are connected to *all* Christians by our belief in the same Father, the same Lord—Jesus Christ—and the same Holy Spirit. As we learn from one another, we come to understand our own stories better and be more-faithful disciples of Jesus Christ.
2. Orthodoxy claims to be the one true church and the tradition that holds most closely to the traditions of the early church.
3. The Orthodox church bases its doctrine on Christ, the Scriptures, and the ecumenical councils that summarized the beliefs of the early church (such as the Nicene Creed).
4. Orthodox Christians place an emphasis on both Scripture and tradition. They consider the early church Fathers as interpreters of the Bible whose writings bear witness to what it means to be a Christian.
5. Orthodox worship is a mystical experience designed to help worshipers "see" divine reality.
   - The dome in many Orthodox churches signifies the cosmos and reminds worshipers of the vastness of God's kingdom and God's presence, which continually surround us.
   - Icons of saints and martyrs remind worshipers that they are surrounded by a great cloud of witnesses.
   - Each service includes the liturgy of the Word (reading from the Holy Scriptures) and the liturgy of the Eucharist, which includes remembering the cross, the tomb, the Resurrection,

the Ascension, and the Second Coming—something yet to happen in earthly terms but already accomplished in mystical terms.

6. Orthodox worship shows us the importance of gathering with other Christians to remember that this is not the real world and that we are surrounded by a great cloud of witnesses, which builds our faith.

Taking It Home

Do some background reading on the Book of Hebrews in a study Bible or Bible commentary. Who was the letter written for and why? Ask yourself: *Am I in danger of wandering from the faith in any way?* Consider what encouragement you may need to persevere in the faith. How might you seek out this encouragement? (If possible, plan to read the entire Book of Hebrews by the end of the week.)

Focus on Hebrews 5:11-14. Note the author's frustration with the lack of spiritual growth of the recipients of this letter. How are you maturing as a Christian? What might you do to grow even more?

The idea of earthly things foreshadowing and pointing toward a heavenly reality is very important in Orthodoxy. Review Hebrews 8–10. What does the author say about how the earthly sanctuary or temple pre-figures the heavenly? How might these chapters shape how we design our permanent sanctuary at resurrection?

Read Hebrews 11, the "hall of faith" chapter, reading on through 12:3. What is the author's point? What helps you to see this life as only a foretaste of the "real world"? How is God calling you to live by faith this week?

CATHOLICISM: SACRAMENT AND MASS

Main Idea: Catholicism reminds us of the importance of ritual, the role of reverence, and the power of the Eucharist.

Getting Started

Session Goals

This session is intended to help participants...

- become familiar with some of the beliefs and practices of the Roman Catholic Church;
- gain a deeper appreciation for ritual and reverence in worship and everyday life;
- better understand the meaning and significance of the Eucharist.

Opening Prayer

Dear God, we come together today to learn about another branch of the Christian family tree, Catholicism. We ask you to remind us that our aim is not to critique the Catholic faith tradition but to learn from it so that our own faith might be enriched. Help us through our study and discussion to become more authentic and effective disciples of your Son, Jesus Christ. We affirm that all who call upon his name are members of one body, one faith. May we be united in spirit, in love, and in service so that your kingdom work may be accomplished in our world. In Jesus' name we pray. Amen.

Biblical Foundation

O come, let us worship and bow down,
  let us kneel before the LORD, *our Maker!*
For he is our God,
  and we are the people of his pasture,
  and the sheep of his hand.

(Psalm 95:6-7)

Jesus said to them, "Very truly, I tell you, unless you eat the flesh of the Son of Man and drink his blood, you have no life in you. Those who eat my flesh and drink my blood have eternal life, and I will raise them up on the last day; for my flesh is true food and my blood is true drink. Those who eat my flesh and drink my blood abide in me, and I in them. (John 6:53-56)

Opening Activity

Ask the group to define the word *ritual*. Write their ideas on a chalkboard or large sheet of paper. Then ask them to name as many different kinds of rituals as they can—everyday rituals such as having a cup of coffee each morning, as well as sacred rituals that might be performed by individuals during the week or by congregations on Sunday morning. List their responses. Discuss: What makes a ritual sacred? In what ways are rituals "life giving"? What prevents a ritual from becoming dead or empty?

Learning Together

Video Presentation

Play the video segment for Week 2, *Catholicism*.
Running Time: 17:02 minutes

Key Insights

1. The word *catholic* means universal. Originally it was used as an adjective describing all Christians. It was not until 1054 that the

23

one holy catholic and apostolic church divided, becoming the Orthodox church and the Roman Catholic Church.

2. For Roman Catholics, the Bible is the starting point for all faith and practice. However, the Catholic Church believes that doctrine is continually being revealed to human beings through the guidance of the Holy Spirit. They call this the deposit of faith. So, in addition to the Bible, Catholic doctrine is based on the teachings of the church and the decisions of councils and bishops as summarized in the *Roman Catholic Catechism.*

3. Catholicism reminds us of three important things:
   • Ritual is important in our lives and in our worship. Rituals bring rhythm and order, focus our attention, prepare our hearts to worship God, shape our souls, and enrich our lives.
   • There is power in reverencing what is sacred. God is holy and is to be revered.
   • The Eucharist (Holy Communion) is a powerful way to express our acceptance of Christ's gift of salvation. Although most Protestants do not believe the bread and wine are actually changed into the body and blood of Christ, as Roman Catholics believe, Protestants do believe that Christ is truly present in the bread and the wine and that by receiving them we are, spiritually, receiving Christ himself.

Leader Extra
Catholic Beliefs and Practices

Mary

Protestants affirm all that is found in the New Testament regarding Mary and honor her as the mother of our Lord. Catholics start with the Scriptures but also look to the traditions and theological arguments that developed around Mary through the centuries to affirm doctrines that Protestants do not accept; namely, that she was immaculately conceived, was perpetually a virgin, and was assumed into heaven at her death (her body not being subject to decay). While

Protestants do not find sufficient support in Scripture for these doctrines, Catholics find seeds of the doctrines in the New Testament and cite what they believe to be Holy Spirit-led traditions and teachings of the church through the centuries as pointing toward the truth of these doctrines.

The Rosary

The rosary is a tool used to recount the stories of Mary and Jesus while offering scriptural words of affirmation and prayer. It includes the "Hail Mary" taken from Luke's Gospel; the Lord's Prayer; the Apostles' Creed; and the recounting of the story of Jesus' life, death, and resurrection. There are four sets of what are called mysteries, and there are five mysteries under each set. The four sets of mysteries are as follows:

1. Joyful mysteries (for example, the birth of Jesus)
2. Sorrowful mysteries (for example, the suffering of Jesus' death)
3. Triumph or glorious mysteries (for example, Jesus' resurrection from the dead and ascension into heaven)
4. Luminous mysteries (for example, Jesus' character, ministry, and teachings)

While Protestants might reject portions of the rosary devoted to extra-biblical stories and the repeating of words of affirmation to Mary, the idea of daily making use of this tool to pray, worship, and recount the Gospel stories would not be inconsistent with Protestant devotional practice.

The Eucharist

For Catholics, the Eucharist is the climactic conclusion and the most-important part of what happens when they gather for worship. Catholics believe that in the midst of the prayer offered by the priest, the bread and wine actually become the body and blood of Christ. This is a doctrine called "transubstantiation."

Generally, Protestants have rejected this idea. Yet here the Catholics, rather than the Protestants, are taking the Bible literally; for this is a very literal reading of what Jesus said in John 6 when he spoke of eating his flesh and drinking his blood. It is also a literal reading of what Paul says in 1 Corinthians 11:29: "For all who eat and drink without discerning the body, eat and drink judgment against themselves."

Catholics believe these passages are to be taken literally; and it is true that very early in the history of the church, Christians embraced this idea. Protestants interpret these words to mean receiving the symbols of bread and wine as representing the body and blood of Christ. They believe that Christ is in some sense present in the bread and the wine and that by receiving them we are, spiritually, receiving Christ himself. In the Eucharist we have an opportunity, in a physical way, to express our acceptance of Christ's gift of salvation. We communicate our need for his mercy, we physically receive him, and we experience God's grace in the eating of this meal.

Demonstrations of Reverence

- If the wine of the Eucharist is not completely consumed by the congregation and priests, it is poured into the ground, just as Christ's blood fell to the ground. The consecrated bread is saved in the tabernacle or fed to the birds; it is never thrown away.
- Worshipers bow the knee when facing the place where the body of Christ is kept.
- When the Gospel is read, worshipers make the sign of the cross on their forehead, lips, and heart, in effect saying, "The Gospel be on my mind, and on my lips, and in my heart."
- Worshipers cross themselves when the name of the Trinity is pronounced, in effect saying, "Father, Son, and Holy Spirit, I am yours. Cover me, fill me, have me."

Group Discussion

Note: More questions are provided than you may have time for. Select those you would like your group to discuss.

1. In addition to the Bible, on what does the Roman Catholic Church base its doctrine? What is their reasoning for looking beyond the Scriptures? Why do they believe that the doctrines of the faith are progressively revealed? What has been the traditional Protestant view on the subject?

2. Dr. Claude Sasso, vice-chancellor of the diocese of Kansas City and Saint Joseph and a respected Catholic educator, has compared the doctrine of the Catholic Church to the development of a human being from embryo to grown adult. Although the DNA remains the same, the individual develops and changes through the years. Similarly, although the building blocks of the Christian faith remain the same, church doctrine develops and changes over time. Discuss your thoughts related to this analogy.

3. Why is ritual important in our lives? What are some of the benefits of observing rituals? What does it mean to say that rituals give our lives and our faith "rhythm"?

4. What are some Catholic rituals you know of? (See Leader Extra: Catholic Beliefs and Practices.) How might these practices provide the benefits of rituals previously discussed?

5. What rituals enrich your own life? What rituals enrich the life and worship of your church? Which rituals of your church, if any, do you think have been borrowed or adapted from the Catholic tradition? Which do you think are unique to Protestantism?

6. How would you define or explain the word *reverence*? What are some ways that Roman Catholics show their reverence for God? (See Leader Extra: Catholic Beliefs and Practices.) Do you believe the Protestant church in general has lost a sense of sacredness? Why or why not?

7. Read Psalm 95:1-7a. What reasons does the psalmist give for reverencing God? How does the psalmist suggest we should show

our reverence? What are some other ways we can show our reverence for God?

8. What is the meaning of the Eucharist for Roman Catholic Christians? How does the Protestant understanding of the Eucharist differ? (See Leader Extra: Catholic Beliefs and Practices.)

9. What have you learned from our study of the Roman Catholic Church that will help to deepen your own faith and experience of God?

Group Activity

Invite a pastor to join your group and lead you in the celebration of the Eucharist as observed by your church. Prior to the group session, ask the pastor to prepare to say a few words about your denomination's belief and practice regarding Holy Communion. (Be sure to provide hymnals or other printed materials including the appropriate congregational responses.)

If serving Holy Communion is not feasible for some reason, read the following aloud: "Ignatius of Antioch, writing in AD 107 on his way to martyrdom, described the Eucharist as 'the medicine of immortality, the antidote against death.'" Discuss: What do you think he meant by this? How might our church help worshipers to remember that Holy Communion is not a mindless ritual but the act of receiving the life of Christ?

Wrapping Up

Taking It Home

Briefly review the Taking It Home application exercises included on the Participant Handout. Encourage participants to complete the activities during the coming week, reminding them that they will not be asked to share any details with the group. The exercises are intended for their private use and are designed to help them get the most out of this study that they possibly can.

Invite those participants who have purchased copies of the participant's book to read Chapter 2 this week as a follow-up to this group session. (Those reading chapters in advance of the group sessions will read Chapter 3 this week.)

Notable Quote

"I fear that many times as Protestants we've set aside any sense of sacredness. . . . I appreciate the fact that when Roman Catholics walk into the sanctuary . . . they look to where the tabernacle is that contains the consecrated bread of the host, the body of Christ, and they . . . kneel before that as a way of honoring Christ."

—Adam Hamilton

Closing Prayer

Lord Jesus, we are so thankful that you have called us your friends and have invited us to have a personal relationship with you. Yet we also humbly acknowledge that you are our King. You are King of kings and Lord of lords. Forgive us for the many times and ways we have failed to reverence you as we should. Teach us truly to honor you as we worship together and as we live our lives day by day. We are grateful for the witness of the Roman Catholic Church, which reminds us of the importance of ritual. Lead us to identify those sacred rituals that will help us to develop a continual awareness of your glorious presence. Fill us now with a sense of awe and wonder so that our very lives may be holy expressions of our reverence and love for you. Amen.

Week 2: Catholicism
Participant Handout

O come, let us worship and bow down,
let us kneel before the Lord, our Maker!
(Psalm 95:6)

Jesus said to them, "Very truly, I tell you, unless you eat the flesh
of the Son of Man and drink his blood, you have no life in you."
(John 6:53)

Key Insights

The word *catholic* means universal. Originally it was used as an adjective describing all Christians. It was not until 1054 that the one holy catholic and apostolic church divided, becoming the Orthodox church and the Roman Catholic Church.

For Roman Catholics, the Bible is the starting point for all faith and practice. However, the Catholic Church believes that doctrine is continually being revealed to human beings through the guidance of the Holy Spirit. So, in addition to the Bible, Catholic doctrine is based on the teachings of the church and the decisions of councils and bishops as summarized in the *Roman Catholic Catechism*.

Catholicism reminds us of three important things:

• Ritual is important in our lives and in our worship. Rituals bring rhythm and order, focus our attention, prepare our hearts to worship God, shape our souls, and enrich our lives.

• There is power in reverencing what is sacred. God is holy and is to be revered.

• The Eucharist (Holy Communion) is a powerful way to express our acceptance of Christ's gift of salvation.

Taking It Home

- The Eucharist (Holy Communion, the Lord's Supper) is the central focus of worship in the Catholic Church. It is believed that the bread and wine become the body and blood of Christ, so that one is receiving Christ himself in this meal. The Eucharist mysteriously makes present the sacrifice of Jesus on the cross that we might accept it as our own. Do your own study on the Lord's Supper as described in the New Testament. Make notes as to what you learn and how God speaks to you through these passages: Matthew 26:17-30; John 6:48-58 (Most believe Jesus is speaking about the Eucharist here.); Acts 2:42 and 2:46 (The "breaking of bread" is thought to be a meal that included the Lord's Supper.); Acts 20:7; 1 Corinthians 10:14-22; 11:17-34.
- Catholics have a very high view of Mary. Read Matthew 12:46-50; Luke 1:26-55; 2:16-19, 25-35; 2:41-51; John 19:25b-27; Acts 1:12-14 (This last passage of Scripture demonstrates that Mary was with the apostles and the other leaders of the church.). What do you learn about Mary in these verses? What example does Mary set for you?
- Catholics are known for an emphasis on the importance of works in our salvation. They do not teach that we are saved by our works but that works both produce saving faith and are closely intertwined with saving faith. Read James 2:14-26. What insights does this passage give you?
- Catholics believe the Bible is our primary authority for faith and practice, but they also recognize that the Holy Spirit speaks through the church and continues to guide us into truth. Read John 14:15-26. What was one role of the Holy Spirit? How did the early church make doctrinal and other decisions? Now read Acts 15:1-35. What was at issue here?

LUTHERANISM: WORD AND FAITH

Main Idea: The Lutheran faith tradition emphasizes the idea that human beings are made right with God not by our works, but by God's work in Jesus Christ.

Getting Started

Session Goals
This session is intended to help participants…
- become familiar with key teachings of Martin Luther, which became foundational principles of the Protestant Reformation and core doctrines of the Lutheran Church;
- recognize that every Christian is called to be in ministry in the world;
- gain a deeper appreciation for the accessibility of the Scriptures and the importance of Bible study;
- better understand the doctrine of justification by faith.

Opening Prayer
Dear God, we come together today to learn about another branch of the Christian family tree, Lutheranism. We ask you to remind us that our aim is not to critique the Lutheran faith tradition but to learn from it so that our own faith might be enriched. Help us through our study and discussion to become more authentic and effective disci-

ples of your Son, Jesus Christ. We affirm that all who call upon his name are members of one body, one faith. May we be united in spirit, in love, and in service so that your kingdom work may be accomplished in our world. In Jesus' name we pray. Amen.

Biblical Foundation

But now, apart from law, the righteousness of God has been disclosed, and is attested by the law and the prophets, the righteousness of God through faith in Jesus Christ for all who believe. For there is no distinction, since all have sinned and fall short of the glory of God; they are now justified by his grace as a gift, through the redemption that is in Christ Jesus. (Romans 3:21-24)

Come to him, a living stone, though rejected by mortals yet chosen and precious in God's sight, and like living stones, let yourselves be built into a spiritual house, to be a holy priesthood, to offer spiritual sacrifices acceptable to God through Jesus Christ. (1 Peter 2:4-5)

Opening Activity

Distribute copies of Participant Handout 1: God's Grace and Our Faith. Discuss: What is your understanding of this passage from Romans? What insights do you find helpful in Martin Luther's remarks? How were Luther's remarks liberating to John Wesley? How is one's faith shaped by one's understanding of God's grace?

Learning Together

Video Presentation
Play the video segment for Week 3, *Lutheranism*.
Running Time: 18:12 minutes

Key Insights
1. By the early 1500s, the Roman Catholic Church had veered off course and was in desperate need of reform. The teachings of

a monk named Martin Luther led to the Protestant Reformation and eventually the Lutheran Church. Today there are more than 82 million Lutherans around the world, and they continue to preach and teach the gospel in much the same way that Luther did.

2. Martin Luther's inner spiritual and emotional turmoil coupled with his displeasure with the church of his day led him to study the Scriptures. As a result, he came to discover that God is a God of mercy and that salvation is a gift that comes not through works, but through faith alone.

3. Luther was infuriated by the preaching of Johann Tetzel, inviting people to ease the suffering of their loved ones in Purgatory by purchasing indulgences. Luther responded by writing ninety-five statements or "theses" and posting them on the Wittenberg Castle Church door. The theses were translated into German, printed on the newly invented printing press, and distributed among the people. This was the spark that ignited the Protestant Reformation.

4. In contrast to the church of Martin Luther's day, which was very clerical-centered, Luther promoted the biblical concept of the priesthood of all believers, which means that every follower of Jesus is called to use his or her gifts in ministry in the world.

5. Luther believed that God speaks to ordinary people through the Bible. He said that the Christian's compass is the Scriptures. Luther translated the Bible from Latin into German and challenged people to read the Scriptures.

6. Luther devised what is known as the *Smaller Catechism* as a tool to help believers begin to know the basics of the faith. This book, which was given to all Lutherans, included the Lord's Prayer, the Ten Commandments, and the Apostles' Creed, along with Luther's commentaries on each and his teachings on the sacraments.

7. A central tenet of Luther's faith was that we are made right with God not on the basis of what we do, but on the basis of God's gift to us in Jesus Christ. Salvation is through faith alone, not works. We must simply trust in God's goodness and mercy.

Leader Extra
Indulgences, Ninety-Five Theses, and the Protestant Reformation

In the early 1500s, the pope was raising funds to erect Saint Peter's Cathedral in Rome. To do so, a number of preachers were commissioned to conduct what was essentially a capital funds campaign. The preachers told people that contributing to this effort would result in prayers offered on behalf of a loved one, in which the church would petition God to accept these acts of devotion (the giving of monetary gifts toward the construction of Saint Peter's and the prayers for the departed loved one) as a way of ensuring that the loved one would spend less time in Purgatory. One of these preachers, a man named Johann Tetzel, spoke in Martin Luther's town.

Tetzel's aggressive appeals to the people infuriated Luther and led him to compose a list of ninety-five statements or "theses" questioning the practice of indulgences and the state of the church in his day. He posted his theses on the doors of the Castle Church in Wittenberg, Germany, on October 31, 1517 (what many people call Halloween, but what Lutherans call Reformation Day). Luther's Ninety-five Theses were reproduced on a relatively new invention, the printing press; and soon his challenge to the church and its practices was spread across the land.

Luther expressed in his writings the frustration that many people were feeling with regard to the state of the church and its abuses. When the church refused to acknowledge its abuses and instead sought to silence Luther, there was a break from the Roman Catholic Church, which Luther deemed apostate; and the Protestant branch of Christianity was born, beginning a movement that came to be called the Protestant Reformation. Within a relatively short period of time, Lutheranism came to be the church of large portions of Germany, Denmark, Sweden, and Norway.

Leader Extra
Sola Scriptura

Luther affirmed what is known as "sola scriptura," or Scripture alone. He came to believe that the Bible was the primary authority in defining the faith and practice of Christians, not the pope or the councils or the church. He believed that Christians were to read the Bible and interpret it with the help of the Holy Spirit. This stood in stark contrast to the church of his day, which taught that giving the Bible to the laity was dangerous and therefore the Bible was to be read and interpreted only by the pope and clergy.

Luther said that if a doctrine could not be demonstrated from the Scriptures, it could not be made binding on the church. This was a radical rejection of the role of the church in shaping doctrine, and it led to a rejection of many of the practices of the Roman Catholic Church.

Group Discussion

Note: More questions are provided than you may have time for. Select those you would like your group to discuss.

1. What was the state of the Roman Catholic Church in Martin Luther's day? How had the church veered off course? Do you believe the church today is off course in any way and, if so, how?

2. What was Martin Luther's picture of God as a child and young man? What struggle did this picture cause within Luther, and what was the result of that struggle? How does God use struggles in our lives to lead us to discover truth? If you are willing, share an example from your own life or the life of someone you know.

3. Why were the people of Martin Luther's day being encouraged to purchase indulgences? What was Luther's objection regarding this practice, and what did he do in response? How did Luther's Ninety-five Theses lead to the Protestant Reformation? (See Leader Extra: Indulgences, Ninety-five Theses, and the Protestant Reformation.)

4. What can we learn from Martin Luther about the importance of taking a stand for our faith? When have you taken a stand for your faith that put you at risk? What happened?

5. How would you explain the priesthood of all believers? Read 1 Peter 2:4-5; Ephesians 4:11-12; Matthew 5:13-16. How do these verses support the idea that each of us is called to be in ministry? How does your church help individuals to recognize and respond to the call to be in ministry? How have you responded to the call?

6. How did Luther's understanding of the Scriptures differ from that of the church in his day? What did Luther mean when he said that the Scriptures are the Christian's compass? How did Luther make a significant contribution to biblical literacy among the laity? How would you rate the biblical literacy of Christians today in general? in your church? In what ways has Bible study—both private and group study—contributed to your own spiritual growth?

7. Luther was stunned to find the number of Christians in his day who did not know the basics of the faith. Do you believe this is true today as well? Why or why not? How would you define the "basics of the faith"? What can the church do to teach these basics more effectively?

8. How would you explain "justification by faith" to someone who does not know of God's grace and mercy? Why was this belief so important to Luther—and to the Protestant Reformation? How has your understanding and experience of God's grace changed through the years? What does it mean to trust in God's grace boldly?

9. Contrast someone who is reared in a home where one or both parents never seem to express love or affirmation, or do so only conditionally (for example, if the child performs well enough in school or athletics), to someone who is reared in a home where the parents demonstrate unconditional love and acceptance. How does this upbringing often affect one's relationship with God?

10. What have you learned from our study of Martin Luther and Lutheranism that will help to deepen your own faith and experience of God?

Group Activity

Say the following aloud: Martin Luther believed that all Christians are ordained, in their baptism, to serve God and to do God's work. Joy is found in responding to God's call. Luther believed that every day, in everything we do, we can respond to God's call on our life. Ask participants to name some of the "mission fields" available to us—in the church as well as in our everyday lives. List these in one column on a chalkboard or large sheet of paper. Then discuss some tangible ways we can be in ministry and share the love of Christ in each of these "mission fields." List these ideas in a second column. Challenge participants to choose one idea they can put into practice this week.

Wrapping Up

Taking It Home

Briefly review the Taking It Home application exercises included on Participant Handout 2. Encourage participants to complete the activities during the coming week, reminding them that they will not be asked to share any details with the group. The exercises are intended for their private use and are designed to help them get the most out of this study that they possibly can.

Invite those participants who have purchased copies of the participant's book to read Chapter 3 this week as a follow-up to this group session. (Those reading chapters in advance of the group sessions will read Chapter 4 this week.)

Notable Quote

"God loves you. God is proud of you. God affirms you. And that's the starting point of your faith. It's not trying to get God to love you by doing enough good stuff. It is trusting in his love and living your life in response." —*Adam Hamilton*

Closing Prayer

Merciful God, thank you for the legacy of Martin Luther and the witness of the Lutheran Church. How grateful we are for the depth of your love and the boundless measure of your mercy. May we always remember that we are your beloved children. Help us to look for ways to be your hands and your voice in this world, to serve you in the church and the world. Lord, create in our hearts a longing to study your Word. May it be for us our compass, a lamp to our feet and a light to our path. In Jesus' name we pray. Amen.

Week 3: Lutheranism
Participant Handout 1

God's Grace and Our Faith

But now, apart from law, the righteousness of God has been disclosed, and is attested by the law and the prophets, the righteousness of God through faith in Jesus Christ for all who believe. For there is no distinction, since all have sinned and fall short of the glory of God; they are now justified by his grace as a gift, through the redemption that is in Christ Jesus. (Romans 3:21-24)

Faith is God's work in us, that changes us and gives new birth from God. (John 1:13). It kills the Old Adam and makes us completely different people. It changes our hearts, our spirits, our thoughts and all our powers. It brings the Holy Spirit with it. Yes, it is a living, creative, active and powerful thing, this faith. . . . Faith is a living, bold trust in God's grace, so certain of God's favor that it would risk death a thousand times trusting in it. Such confidence and knowledge of God's grace makes you happy, joyful and bold in your relationship to God and all creatures. The Holy Spirit makes this happen through faith.[1]

—Martin Luther

In the evening I went very unwillingly to a society in Aldersgate Street, where one was reading Luther's preface to the Epistle to the Romans. About a quarter before nine, while he was describing the change which God works in the heart through faith in Christ, I felt my heart strangely warmed. I felt I did trust in Christ, Christ alone, for salvation; and an assurance was given me that He had taken away my sins, even mine, and saved me from the law of sin and death.[2]

—John Wesley

1. From "An Introduction to St. Paul's Letter to the Romans," in Luther's German Bible of 1522 by Martin Luther; translated by Reverend Robert E. Smith.
2. From *The Works of John Wesley,* edited by Albert C. Outler (Abingdon Press, 1988); Vol. 18; entry for May 24, 1738.

Week 3: Lutheranism
Participant Handout 2

[We are] justified by his grace as a gift, through the redemption that is in Christ Jesus. (Romans 3:24)

Let yourselves be built into a spiritual house, to be a holy priest-hood, to offer spiritual sacrifices acceptable to God through Jesus Christ. (1 Peter 2:5)

Key Insights

1. By the early 1500s, the Roman Catholic Church was in desperate need of reform. The teachings of a monk named Martin Luther led to the Protestant Reformation and eventually the Lutheran Church. Today there are more than 82 million Lutherans around the world, and they continue to preach and teach the gospel in much the same way that Luther did.
2. Martin Luther's inner spiritual and emotional turmoil coupled with his displeasure with the church of his day led him to study the Scriptures. As a result, he came to discover that God is a God of mercy and that salvation is a gift that comes not through works, but through faith alone.
3. Luther was infuriated by the preaching of Johann Tetzel, inviting people to ease the suffering of their loved ones in Purgatory by pur-chasing indulgences. He responded by writing ninety-five state-ments or "theses" and posting them on the Wittenberg Castle Church door. The theses were translated into German, printed on the newly invented printing press, and distributed among the people. This was the spark that ignited the Protestant Reformation.
4. Luther promoted the biblical concept of the priesthood of all believers, which means that every follower of Jesus is called to use his or her gifts in ministry in the world.
5. Luther believed that God speaks to ordinary people through the

Bible. He said that the Christian's compass is the Scriptures. Luther translated the Bible from Latin into German and challenged people to read the Scriptures.

6. Luther devised what is known as the *Smaller Catechism* as a tool to help believers begin to know the basics of the faith. It included the Lord's Prayer, the Ten Commandments, and the Apostles' Creed, along with Luther's commentaries on each and his teachings on the sacraments.

7. A central tenet of Luther's faith was that we are made right with God not on the basis of what we do, but on the basis of God's gift to us in Jesus Christ. Salvation is through faith alone. We must simply trust in God's goodness and mercy.

Taking It Home

• Read Romans 3:9–4:3. What does this passage mean for you? What is the difference between accepting God's gift of salvation by faith and then living a grateful life in response, versus trying to win God's approval and salvation by performing good works? Now read Romans 5:1-11. Have you put your trust in God's grace and love? Thank God for the gift of salvation he has already given you through Christ.

• Luther believed that truth must be determined by studying the Scripture. In this he was following the example of the Beroeans of the Acts of the Apostles. Read Acts 17:10-12. How did the Beroeans seek to determine if Paul's preaching was true? Now read 2 Timothy 3:14-17. Here Paul challenges Timothy to read and study the Scriptures. Why? Read a passage of Scripture and invite God to speak to you through it. Begin a journal in which you record what God is showing you through the Word.

• Read 1 Peter 2:4-5. What does this passage say about all Christians? Now read Ephesians 4:11-13. What is the purpose of pastors, teachers, and apostles? What are God's people to be doing? How are you using the gifts God has given you to do the work of ministry?

PRESBYTERIANISM: THE SOVEREIGNTY OF GOD

Main Idea: A hallmark of Presbyterian theology is the sovereignty of God—the idea that God reigns over every aspect of creation.

Getting Started

Session Goals

This session is intended to help participants...

* understand the beginnings of the Reformed and Presbyterian traditions;
* become familiar with some key Calvinist beliefs;
* examine various positions on the doctrines of predestination and the sovereignty of God;
* recognize the redemptive plan and power of God at work in the world and in our lives.

Opening Prayer

Dear God, we come together today to learn about another branch of the Christian family tree, Presbyterianism. We ask you to keep us mindful that our aim is not to critique the Presbyterian faith tradition but to learn from it so that our own faith might be enriched. Help us through our study and discussion to become more authentic and effective disciples of your Son, Jesus Christ. We affirm that all who call upon his name are members of one body, one faith. May we be united in spirit, in love, and in service so that your kingdom work may be accomplished in our world. In Jesus' name we pray. Amen.

Biblical Foundation

> *For I know that my Redeemer lives,*
> *and that at the last he will stand upon the earth;*
> *and after my skin has been thus destroyed,*
> *then in my flesh I shall see God,*
> *whom I shall see on my side,*
> *and my eyes shall behold, and not another.*
> *(Job 19:25-27a)*

> *In your book were written*
> *all the days that were formed for me,*
> *when none of them as yet existed.*
> *How weighty to me are your thoughts, O God!*
> *How vast is the sum of them!*
> *I try to count them—they are more than the sand;*
> *I come to the end—I am still with you.*
> *(Psalm 139:16b-18)*

> *We know that all things work together for good for those who love God, who are called according to his purpose. (Romans 8:28)*

Opening Activity

Ask participants to give quick answers to the following question: What does it mean to say that God is sovereign? Write the responses on a chalkboard or large sheet of paper. Briefly discuss: Is there a difference between believing that God wills or instigates everything that happens and believing that God knows everything that will happen and is able to fold everything into his plans and purposes?

44

Learning Together

Video Presentation
Play the video segment for Week 4, *Presbyterianism.*
Running Time: 14:07 minutes

Key Insights
1. Some of the reformers who came after Luther, such as John Calvin, believed that Luther was on the right track but that he did not go far enough. Luther believed that any church practice that was forbidden or contradicted in the New Testament should be thrown out; later reformers believed that if the New Testament did not point to a particular church practice, it should be thrown out. They saw themselves as bringing the church even more in line with the apostolic traditions.
2. Calvin put the theology of the Reformation into a systematic form. At age twenty-six he wrote the first edition of his book *Institutes of the Christian Religion,* which perhaps was the most-important book produced during the Protestant Reformation. Calvin's teachings are at the center of the Calvinist, Reformed, and Presbyterian traditions. (See Leader Extra: John Calvin and John Knox.)
3. Two general characteristics of Presbyterians:
   - Presbyterians place an emphasis on experiencing God's grace—a moment of conversion or recognition.
   - Presbyterians tend to be a bit "cerebral," loving God with their minds through theological and biblical meditation and reflection.
4. Calvin's theology can be summarized in the five points of Calvinism (TULIP):
   T Total depravity: Human beings are born into sin and cannot save themselves.
   U Unconditional election: There are some people who were elected or chosen by God before the foundation of the earth to be God's people, to be saved—not by their merit, but by God's

sovereign choice. Others were chosen for eternal damnation. (Note: Many Presbyterians today distance themselves from this doctrine of predestination.)

L Limited Atonement: Jesus' death on the cross atones for the sins of the elect only, not for the sins of those who are not elect.

I Irresistible grace: If you are elect, God has chosen you from the foundation of the earth; there is nothing you can do to resist God's grace.

P Perseverance of the saints: If you are elect or chosen by God for salvation, there is no way you can lose your salvation.

5. Many Presbyterians today distance themselves from the doctrine of predestination. Some say God knows in advance who will choose him; and so, by virtue of knowing this in advance, God has elected or chosen them. Others say God is sovereign and election is a mystery we really cannot understand.

6. The word *Presbyterian* comes from the Greek word *presbuteros*, which means "elders." The organization of the Presbyterian Church does not include bishops but includes elders who lead each local congregation. (There are teaching elders, who are the pastors; and there are lay elders, who are the lay leadership of the church.)

7. A primary emphasis of Presbyterianism is God's sovereignty. Some Presbyterians take a strong stance regarding God's sovereignty, stating that nothing happens outside of God's will. Others say that although God knows everything, not everything happens according to his will. In other words, God does not cause evil but folds everything that happens into his purposes; nothing is outside God's redemptive plan and power.

8. God is constantly working in our lives. God has a will for each of our lives and wants to fold us into his purposes and plans every day.

Leader Extra
John Calvin and John Knox

John Calvin, born in 1509, was eight years old when Luther posted his Ninety-five Theses on the doors of the Castle Church at Wittenberg, signaling the beginning of the Reformation. Calvin studied law in Paris and in his early twenties had a conversion experience. At age twenty-five he left Paris for Basel, Switzerland, where he became an avowed Protestant seeking the reform of the church. A year later, he wrote the first edition of *Institutes of the Christian Religion,* perhaps the single most-important book published during the Reformation, and a book he would continue to revise for the next twenty-five years.

John Calvin and his protégé John Knox were among the second wave of reformers who felt that Luther had not gone far enough in calling for reform in the church, and their efforts resulted in the formation of the Reformed and Presbyterian churches. (Swiss, Dutch, and some German groups used the name "Reformed," while Scotch and English groups used the name "Presbyterian.") Knox played a key role in forming the Church of Scotland, which Presbyterians view as their mother church; but Calvin is seen as the theological father of both the Presbyterian and Reformed traditions.

Leader Extra
Predestination and God's Sovereignty

Predestination

There are several passages in the Bible that speak of God having predestined persons to become his followers, such as Ephesians 1:3-14. Some translations use the word *predestined* in verses 5 and 11, while others use the word *destined*. Some believe this passage teaches that God chose specific people to be saved before the world began; these are the "elect." John Calvin taught that those who were not elect God predestined for damnation and that neither the elect nor the damned could do anything to change their status.

Others understand the word *predestined* to mean that God knew in advance who would choose him, not that God chose in advance who would be saved. Romans 8:29 seems to reflect this idea. Still others believe that God's choosing, God's election, and God's predestination described in Ephesians 1 is more general than specific—that God predestined that all those who would accept Christ would be holy, loved, and adopted as his children. Much of the Bible seems to indicate that "as many as received Christ" could be saved, which seems to line up with the idea that God, by his grace, gives persons the opportunity to respond to the gospel but some reject his offer of life.

God's Sovereignty

Presbyterians typically hold a very high view of the sovereignty of God. Part of the word *sovereignty* is the word *reign*. The idea is that God does what God chooses. Calvin taught that nothing happens apart from the will of God. Tragedies, suffering, and even horrible things that humans do to one another ultimately are part of God's working in the world. Humans do evil, but God is ultimately in charge of what is happening on a daily basis; and so the evil we do to one another is also part of God's will in our lives.

For some, this brings great comfort. No matter what kind of terrible thing happens in our lives, it is God's will; and since God is holy and good, there must be a plan we cannot see that is at work. Others find this idea disturbing, believing it seems to attribute human evil (and every natural disaster) ultimately to God. Many Christians tend to think of God's sovereignty as meaning that God is ultimately in control but that God has allowed the world to be subjected to human beings, who often live in rebellion against God's will. Thus, the evil that happens in the world is generally not God's will but a result of humanity's sin. Even so, God takes all that happens in our lives and, when we place it in his hands, uses it for his glory and purposes.

Dr. Tom Are, Senior Pastor of Village Presbyterian Church in Prairie Village, Kansas, notes that although he does not believe God causes evil or natural disasters, nothing is outside God's ultimate scope of influence. He comments, "Nothing . . . is beyond the redemptive grace of God; and in that sense God is sovereign. All the evil we see in the world would seem to bear witness that God is not powerful, but the doctrine of sovereignty says that God is more powerful than these signs of evil and that God will ultimately fold these into his purposes. Whether we're talking about natural disaster or the terrible things we do to one another, God will not let evil and destruction be the last word."

Tom Are's interpretation of divine sovereignty is one on which both Calvinists and non-Calvinists would be likely to agree.

Group Discussion

Note: More questions are provided than you may have time for. Select those you would like your group to discuss.

1. How did later reformers differ from Luther regarding their views on determining the validity of church practices? How did this difference impact the Protestant Reformation?

2. Who was John Calvin, and what role did he play in the Protestant Reformation? What were his major contributions or accomplishments? Who was John Knox, and what was his role in the formation of the Presbyterian Church? (See Leader Extra: John Calvin and John Knox.)

3. What was the significance of Calvin's *Institutes of the Christian Religion?* Why is this book particularly important to the Reformed and Presbyterian traditions?

4. How did Dr. Doug Rumford, a pastor in the Presbyterian Church of America, characterize Presbyterians? Would you agree with this general characterization? Why or why not?

5. What is the meaning of the word *Presbyterian*, and what does this teach us about the Presbyterian Church?

6. Briefly review and discuss the five distinctive beliefs of historic Presbyterianism known by the acronym TULIP. Do all Presbyterians today hold fast to these ideas? Where do you agree and disagree with these ideas?

7. How would you define or explain the historical Calvinist doctrine of predestination? What are some of the objections to the doctrine of predestination? Does this doctrine raise any difficulties for you personally? Why or why not? Describe a more-moderate understanding of the idea of predestination or election. What response would Christ have Christians on opposite sides of the issue take toward one another? (See Leader Extra: Predestination and God's Sovereignty.)

8. Compare and contrast a conservative understanding of the doctrine of God's sovereignty with a more-moderate understanding of this doctrine. On what point (or points) might Calvinists and non-Calvinists be likely to agree? (See Leader Extra: Predestination and God's Sovereignty.)

9. What does it mean to say that God is sovereign in *your* life? How should this affect the way you live your life each day?

10. What have you learned from our study of Calvinism and Presbyterianism that will help to deepen your own faith and experience of God?

Group Activity

Divide the class into two groups. Ask one group to read Psalm 46 and the other group to read Psalm 139. Have each group discuss and record any insights the psalm gives them regarding the sovereignty of God. Then come back together and ask one person from each group to share their findings with the class.

Wrapping Up

Taking It Home

Briefly review the Taking It Home application exercises included on the Participant Handout. Encourage participants to complete the activities during the coming week, reminding them that they will not be asked to share any details with the group. The exercises are intended for their private use and are designed to help them get the most out of this study that they possibly can.

Invite those participants who have purchased copies of the participant's book to read Chapter 4 this week as a follow-up to this group session. (Those reading chapters in advance of the group sessions will read Chapter 5 this week.)

Notable Quote

"God wants to use you every day and fold you into his purposes and plans. The problem is, most of us aren't listening very carefully. . . . The prayer I encourage you to pray every day is just to yield yourself to God and say, 'God, use me today. Help me to honor and glorify you in some way.' "

—*Adam Hamilton*

Closing Prayer

O God, thank you for the witness of John Calvin and the Presbyterian Church. We are so grateful that you are sovereign of the universe. We long to follow you and serve you. Each day help us to open ourselves to your will—to look and listen to see how we can be useful to you and bring glory to your name. Show us the people who need us to encourage them. Help us to watch and listen. Some in this room right now are experiencing trials and are troubled and afraid. And yet your sovereignty reminds us that their lives are in your hands. You make all things work together for good for those who are called according to your purpose. Help us to trust you with all our hearts. In Jesus' name we pray. Amen.

Week 4: Presbyterianism
Participant Handout

We know that all things work together for good for those who love God, who are called according to his purpose. (Romans 8:28)

Key Insights

1. Some of the reformers who came after Luther, such as John Calvin, believed that Luther was on the right track but that he did not go far enough. They believed that if the New Testament did not point to a particular church practice, it should be thrown out. They saw themselves as bringing the church even more in line with the apostolic traditions.

2. Calvin put the theology of the Reformation into a systematic form. His teachings are at the center of the Calvinist, Reformed, and Presbyterian traditions.

3. Two general characteristics of Presbyterians:
   - Presbyterians place an emphasis on experiencing God's grace—a moment of conversion or recognition.
   - Presbyterians tend to be a bit "cerebral," loving God with their minds through theological and biblical meditation and reflection.

4. Calvin's theology can be summarized in the five points of Calvinism (TULIP):

   T Total depravity: Human beings are born into sin and cannot save themselves.

   U Unconditional election: There are some people who were elected or chosen by God before the foundation of the earth to be saved; others were chosen for eternal damnation.

   L Limited atonement: Jesus' death on the cross atones for the sins of the elect only.

   I Irresistible grace: If you are elect, God has chosen you from the foundation of the earth; there is nothing you can do to resist God's grace.

   P Perseverance of the saints: If you are chosen by God for salvation, you cannot lose your salvation.

5. Many Presbyterians today distance themselves from the doctrine of predestination. Some say God knows in advance who will choose him; and so, by virtue of knowing this in advance, God has elected or chosen them. Others say God is sovereign and election is a mystery we really cannot understand.

6. "Presbyterian" comes from the Greek word *presbuteros*, which means "elders." The organization of the Presbyterian Church does not include bishops; elders lead each congregation.

7. A primary emphasis of Presbyterianism is God's sovereignty. Some Presbyterians take a strong stance regarding God's sovereignty, stating that nothing happens outside of God's will. Others say that God does not cause evil but folds everything that happens into his purposes.

8. God has a will for each of our lives and wants to fold us into his purposes and plans every day.

Taking It Home

Most Calvinists and non-Calvinists would agree that God takes all that happens in our lives and, when we place it in his hands, uses it for his glory and purposes. This week we will focus on this idea.

- Read Psalm 103. What does this psalm say about how God reigns?
- Read Job 19:25-27a. Why do you think that Job, who lost everything, continued to trust in God? What does a strong trust in God's rule and reign produce in us?
- Read Lamentations 3:19-33. What do these verses tell us about God? What gives us hope even in the worst of times?
- Read Philippians 1. What was the apostle Paul's perspective on his own suffering? How does his view of God's reign and work in our lives—even in adversity—help you?
- Read Romans 8:28. How does this promise sustain you in difficult times? Read Psalm 25:1-10; Proverbs 3:5-6; Isaiah 12. What does it mean for *you* to trust in the Lord? In what ways do you need to trust in the Lord right now?

ANGLICANISM: COMMON PRAYER

Main Idea: *The Anglican tradition reminds us that the essence of the Christian faith is found in prayer and worship.*

Getting Started

Session Goals
This session is intended to help participants...
- become familiar with the history of the English Reformation and the beginnings of the Anglican and Episcopalian traditions;
- become familiar with some of the characteristics or marks of the Anglican tradition;
- recognize the significance of the Book of Common Prayer in the Anglican tradition;
- recognize the centrality of prayer in the Christian life.

Opening Prayer
Dear God, we come together today to learn about another branch of the Christian family tree, Anglicanism. We ask you to keep us mindful that our aim is not to critique the Anglican faith tradition but to learn from it so that our own faith might be enriched. Help us through our study and discussion to become more authentic and effective disciples of your Son, Jesus Christ. We affirm that all who

call upon his name are members of one body, one faith. May we be united in spirit, in love, and in service so that your kingdom work may be accomplished in our world. In Jesus' name we pray. Amen.

Biblical Foundation

Seven times a day I praise you
for your righteous ordinances.
(Psalm 119:164)

But now more than ever the word about Jesus spread abroad; many crowds would gather to hear him and to be cured of their diseases. But he would withdraw to deserted places and pray.
(Luke 5:15-16)

Rejoice always, pray without ceasing, give thanks in all circumstances; for this is the will of God in Christ Jesus for you.
(1 Thessalonians 5:16-18)

Opening Activity

Have someone read aloud 1 Thessalonians 5:16-18. Discuss: What does Paul mean when he instructs us to "pray without ceasing" and to "give thanks in all circumstances"? How can we do this? Now have someone read aloud Philippians 4:6-7. Discuss: How would your life be different if you turned every worry into a prayer? What hinders you from doing this? What has been your experience in those times when you have spent your time praying instead of worrying?

Learning Together

Video Presentation

Play the video segment for Week 5, *Anglicanism*.
Running Time: 16:19 minutes

Key Insights

1. As on the continent of Europe, earnest people of faith were calling for reform in the Catholic Church in England. However, it was a king's desire for an heir that ultimately led the English church to split from the Roman Catholic Church and become the Church of England. For a brief summary of the English Reformation, see Leader Extra: Reformation in England.

2. Marks of the Anglican Church include the following:
   - Threefold ministry (bishop, priest, deacon)
   - The seven sacraments, with particular emphasis on Holy Baptism and Holy Eucharist
   - Sense of reverence in liturgy
   - Reliance upon the spiritual disciplines
   - Bishops, priests, and deacons can be married; and, in most parts of the communion (including the U.S.), they can be women
   - Laity share in the ministry of the church

3. Anglicans determine what they believe and practice by what is called the three-legged stool of Anglicanism: 1) Scripture, 2) tradition, and 3) reason.

4. After the Bible, the most-important book in the Anglican tradition is the Book of Common Prayer, which includes several "offices" (morning, noonday, and evening prayer, as well as the office of compline, which is said just before going to bed), a daily two-year lectionary that takes you through the Psalms and various lessons of both Testaments, and corporate prayers.

5. The Anglican tradition reminds us *lex orandi, lex credendi,* which means "the law of prayer is the law of belief"—in other words, as we pray, so we believe. What we pray and how we pray shapes what we believe. Prayer, praise, and worship are the most-important things we do.

Leader Extra

Reformation in England

- One of the first voices calling for reform in the church in England was John Wycliffe, who lived 150 years before Martin Luther. Over the next 150 years, there were other voices, including William Tyndale, who translated a new version of the Bible from Latin into English.
- Catherine of Aragon's inability to provide King Henry VIII with a male heir, coupled with the king's romantic interest in Anne Boleyn, led him to seek an annulment of his marriage, which the pope refused to grant. The king married Ann Boleyn without the pope's annulment of his previous marriage, and the pope responded by excommunicating him. In turn, the king and Parliament declared that the pope was no longer the head of the Church of England. The Church of England continued to be Catholic; but its authority came from England, not Rome.
- After Henry's death, his son Edward VI came to the throne and led the church in a Protestant direction, largely guided by influential Protestants (primarily Calvinists). During his reign, clergy were allowed to marry; and the first Book of Common Prayer, a book in the language of the people for daily prayers and worship, was prepared.
- When Edward died at age sixteen, his half-sister Mary came to the throne. She held strong Catholic convictions and sought to reverse the Protestant reforms and to bring the Church of England back under the authority of Rome. In twenty-five years, England had gone from being Roman Catholic to English Catholic to Calvinistic Protestant and back to Roman Catholic.
- A few years later Mary died, and her half-sister Elizabeth came to the throne. Recognizing the possibility of religious civil war, she tried to navigate a middle way (*via media*) between Catholicism and Protestantism, with the theology of the church drawing from both traditions.
- After Elizabeth's death, her brother James inherited the throne. He

rejected both Protestantism and Catholicism, so he clung to what was an Anglican tradition—the center of the faith. He authorized a new translation of the Bible that represented a middle way between Protestantism and Catholicism, the King James Bible.

Leader Extra
About the Episcopal Church

The Anglican Church in the United States is known as the Episcopal Church. Episcopal worship looks more Catholic than that of other Protestant churches. Like Roman Catholics and Orthodox Christians, Episcopalians worship with all their senses. They use their bodies to bow and to cross themselves, they listen to words and music, they smell the incense, they see the light of candles, and they taste the bread and wine of the Eucharist. The Episcopal Church embraces a view of Holy Communion very close to that of Catholicism. Episcopalians believe in two Gospel sacraments (Holy Communion and baptism) but view the other five Roman Catholic sacraments as "sacramental rites." The Episcopal Church allows clergy to marry, emphasizes the priesthood of all believers, and looks to the Scriptures as its primary basis for faith and practice.

Leader Extra
Praying the Hours

As with the Catholic tradition of the Benedictines, Anglicans invite us to consider setting aside certain times of the day to commune with God through prayer, worship, and reading the Psalms. Anglicans also invite us to "pray the hours"—at least two or three set times or offices of prayer every day. The pattern is to begin each day in prayer and reading the Psalms. The morning daily office is called "lauds," which means praise. When you awaken, you pause to praise God and place your life in his hands, to invite him to guide, lead, use, and walk with you throughout the day. At noon you pause in the middle of your day for what is known as "sext," named for the sixth hour of the day. Here you reset your spiritual compass. You pause to pray, to give thanks for the morning, and to ask for grace for the afternoon; and you read another psalm. Then at sunset you observe another time of prayer and worship, called "vespers." The final time of prayer for the day is "compline," which comes from the Latin for "to complete," since this time of prayer completes the day. At this time you pause to thank God for the day and examine what you have done, inviting God to help you see where you sinned or fell short of his plans and to teach you how to live more according to his will the following day. Once again you read a psalm.

Anglicans call us to bring discipline and order to our prayer lives. They invite us to have multiple times of prayer and praise and worship each day; at least two or three are suggested as a minimum. They maintain that doing this really does make all the difference.

Group Discussion

Note: More questions are provided than you may have time for. Select those you would like your group to discuss.

1. What ultimately led the English Church to split from the Roman Catholic Church and become the Church of England? Do you find any details of the history of the English Reformation surprising or shocking? Why or why not? (See Leader Extra: Reformation in England.)

2. How did Queen Elizabeth try to navigate a "middle way"? Do you feel this was a wise thing to do? (See Leader Extra: Reformation in England.)

3. In what ways is the Anglican Church similar to the Roman Catholic Church? In what ways is it similar to the Protestant tradition?

4. How has the Anglican Church historically determined what they believe and practice?

5. What is the Book of Common Prayer, and what significance does it have in the Anglican tradition? What does it include? How is it used?

6. If you did not do the Opening Activity, read 1 Thessalonians 5:16-18. What does Paul mean when he instructs us to "pray without ceasing" and "give thanks in all circumstances"? How can we do this?

7. Why do Anglicans—and other Christians—set aside certain times of the day to commune with God through prayer, worship, and reading the Psalms? What benefits might result from such a practice? What are some of the hindrances or obstacles you might face if you were to adopt this practice? How might you overcome them?

8. Why is a disciplined prayer life important? What happens when we neglect our prayer lives? Share from your own experiences, as you are willing.

9. What do we learn from the Gospels about Jesus' practices of prayer? Scan the Gospels to find examples of times and places Jesus prayed. Why do you think Jesus took the time to pray?

10. What have you learned from our study of Anglicanism that will help to deepen your own faith and experience of God?

Group Activity

Divide the class into groups of three to five. Say: Episcopalians call us to bring discipline and order to our prayer lives. They invite us to have multiple times of prayer and praise and worship each day. They maintain that doing this really does make all the difference. Take turns now sharing some of the disciplines or habits that have made a difference in your own prayer life. How have these practices benefited you?

Wrapping Up

Taking It Home

Briefly review the Taking It Home application exercises included on the Participant Handout. Encourage participants to complete the activities during the coming week, reminding them that they will not be asked to share any details with the group. The exercises are intended for their private use and are designed to help them get the most out of this study that they possibly can.

Invite those participants who have purchased copies of the participant's book to read Chapter 5 this week as a follow-up to this group session. (Those reading chapters in advance of the group sessions will read Chapter 6 this week.)

Notable Quote
"We can know all the right stuff up here [in our minds]; but if we're not praying and yielding ourselves to the work of the Holy Spirit, we will utterly miss the mark. It's in the life of prayer . . . that our lives are transformed into the image of Christ."

—*Adam Hamilton*

Closing Prayer
Lord God, thank you for the witness of the Anglican and Episcopalian traditions which remind us of the importance of daily prayer and worship. We confess that sometimes days go by when we have not approached you in prayer—when we have not stopped to reflect on and try to understand your will. Often we feel empty and drained—all because we have not carried everything to you in prayer. Teach us to pray the Psalms. Teach us to pause in the middle of our busy days to offer our lives to you and invite your Spirit to work in us. Help us to be people of prayer and praise and worship. In Jesus' name we pray. Amen.

Week 5: Anglicanism
Participant Handout

Rejoice always, pray without ceasing, give thanks in all circumstances; for this is the will of God in Christ Jesus for you.

(1 Thessalonians 5:16-18)

Key Insights

1. As on the continent of Europe, earnest people of faith were calling for reform in the Catholic Church in England. However, it was a king's desire for an heir that ultimately led the English church to split from the Roman Catholic Church and become the Church of England. For a brief summary of the English Reformation, see Leader Extra: Reformation in England.

2. Marks of the Anglican Church include the following:
   • Threefold ministry (bishop, priest, deacon)
   • The seven sacraments, with particular emphasis on Holy Baptism and Holy Eucharist
   • Sense of reverence in liturgy
   • Reliance upon the spiritual disciplines
   • Bishops, priests, and deacons can be married; and, in most parts of the communion (including the U.S.), they can be women
   • Laity share in the ministry of the church

3. The "three-legged stool of Anglicanism" identifies how they determine what they believe and practice: 1) Scripture, 2) tradition, and 3) reason.

4. After the Bible, the most-important book in the Anglican tradition is the Book of Common Prayer, which includes several "offices" (morning, noonday, and evening prayer, as well as the office of compline, which is said just before going to bed), a daily two-year lectionary that takes you through the Psalms and various lessons of both Testaments, and corporate prayers.

5. The Anglican tradition reminds us *lex orandi, lex credendi,* which means "the law of prayer is the law of belief"—in other words, as we pray, so we believe. What we pray and how we pray shapes what we believe. Prayer, praise, and worship are the most-important things we do.

Taking It Home

Choose three days this week when you can observe three of the daily offices of prayer from the Episcopal tradition: morning, midday, and bedtime prayers.

Day 1

Lauds (morning): Begin with a prayer of thanksgiving for the day. Read Psalm 1. Pray that you might be like the one who delights in the law of the Lord. Read Matthew 5:13-16 and pray that you might be salt and light today. Invite God to guide and use you today. Lift up your needs to the Lord. Conclude your prayer time with the Lord's Prayer.

Sext (midday): Give thanks for your meal and for the morning that has passed. Read Psalm 2. Focus on the final line of this psalm. What does this mean for you?

Compline (bedtime): Thank God for the day and its blessings. Pause to consider anything for which you need God's forgiveness or help in order to learn from your experiences and live differently tomorrow. Read Psalm 3 aloud, focusing on verses 3-5.

Day 2

Lauds (morning): Begin with a prayer of thanksgiving for the day; then read Psalm 5. How do verses 4-6 call you to live today? Read again verses 11-12 and pray that you might be like the one who takes refuge in God.

Sext (midday): Give thanks for your meal and for the morning that has passed. Read Psalm 6. Have you ever felt as the psalmist does in this prayer? Note the confidence of verse 9.

Compline (bedtime): Thank God for the day and its blessings. Pause to consider anything in the day for which you need God's forgiveness or help in order to learn from your experiences and live differently tomorrow. Read Psalm 4 aloud. Are there any false gods in your life? Note that the psalm begins with the psalmist in distress; what has changed in verse 8?

Day 3

Lauds (morning): Begin with a prayer of thanksgiving for the day and for God's goodness; then read Psalm 9:1-11. How do verses 1 and 2 call you to live today? Pray that God will help you live these words today. Lift up your concerns to God.

Sext (midday): Give thanks for your meal and for the morning that has passed. Read Psalm 7:1-10. Have you ever felt as though enemies were seeking to wound you? Invite God to search your mind and be your shield; then read aloud verse 17.

Compline (bedtime): Thank God for the day and its blessings. Pause to consider anything in the day for which you need God's forgiveness or help in order to learn from your experiences and live differently tomorrow. Step outside and look up at the stars; then read Psalm 8 aloud.

BAPTISTS:
BAPTISM, CONVERSION, AND SCRIPTURE

Main Idea: The Baptist faith tradition reminds us of the importance of reading God's Word, having a personal relationship with Jesus Christ, and sharing our faith in Christ with others.

Getting Started

Session Goals
This session is intended to help participants . . .
- become familiar with the beginnings of the Baptist tradition;
- understand some of the beliefs and practices of Baptists;
- recognize three primary emphases of all Baptists;
- appreciate the value of three qualities demonstrated by Baptists.

Opening Prayer
Dear God, we come together today to learn about another branch of the Christian family tree, Baptists. We ask you to keep us mindful that our aim is not to critique the Baptist faith tradition but to learn from it so that our own faith might be enriched. Help us through our study and discussion to become more authentic and effective disciples of your Son, Jesus Christ. We affirm that all who call upon his name are members of one body, one faith. May we be united in spirit, in love, and in service so that your

kingdom work may be accomplished in our world. In Jesus' name we pray. Amen.

Biblical Foundation

For God so loved the world that he gave his only Son, so that everyone who believes in him may not perish but may have eternal life. (John 3:16)

For the wages of sin is death, but the free gift of God is eternal life in Christ Jesus our Lord. (Romans 6:23)

Opening Activity

Invite participants to share their responses to this question: How has the Bible been an important "road map" in your life? Follow-up questions: How has Bible study shaped your understanding of God? impacted your personal relationship with Jesus Christ? affected your spiritual growth?

Learning Together

Video Presentation

Play the video segment for Week 6, *Baptists*.
Running Time: 15:39 minutes

Key Insights

1. In the 1600s, there were many who were dissatisfied with the middle path of the Church of England. They sought to purge the church of its Catholic or "high church" elements; to restore it to what they believed was its New Testament character; and to purify the church and its members, challenging them to lead a holy life. This group became known as "Puritans" because they emphasized moral and spiritual purity.
2. Many of the Puritans remained part of the Church of England, seeking to work for change from within. The more-radical

Puritans left the church; among these were the Pilgrims. Another group of Puritans who called for more-radical reform and eventually left the church were the Baptists.

3. Baptists believed that only those practices explicitly described in the New Testament were to be made normative for the church. Since the New Testament only reports the baptism of adult converts who were called to repent and be baptized, it was reasoned that infant baptism should be eliminated. Thus they were first called Anapedopbaptist, which refers to those against the baptism of infants.

4. John Smyth was the first Baptist pastor on record. He established his church in 1609, and on the first Sunday he rebaptized all the adults who had been baptized as infants.

5. Baptists rejected anything in church practice that appeared "Catholic," such as the liturgical elements of worship, the formal acts of worship, and the vestments or dress of the clergy. (See Leader Extra: Distinctive Differences.)

6. Because Baptists were seen as radical reformers, they were persecuted by both the Puritans and the Church of England. Consequently, Baptists have traditionally had a strong appreciation for the separation of church and state.

7. There are many different varieties of Baptists, including American Baptist, Southern Baptist, Free Will Baptist, and a whole host of others. Baptists do not form denominations. Instead, the autonomy of a given Baptist church is protected. Baptist churches do associate with other churches that are like-minded in order to pursue common goals; these associations are called conventions (for example, Northern Baptist Convention, Southern Baptist Convention).

8. Three core beliefs or emphases of Baptists:
   1) The inspiration, infallibility, and preservation of Scripture
   2) The importance of one's personal relationship with God
   3) Salvation by grace through faith alone
   (For more on Baptist beliefs, see Leader Extra: Basic Beliefs and Practices.)

9. Baptists demonstrate three qualities other Protestant groups can learn from:
   1) A love of God's Word and Bible study
   2) An emphasis on missions and evangelism
   3) The simple salvation message

Leader Extra
Distinctive Differences

- Because Baptists rejected anything in the church that appeared "Catholic," Baptist worship services have not traditionally included such things as processionals, acolytes, cross bearers, or candles.
- Baptist churches have no altar, which is a place of sacrifice, because Baptists do not hold the Catholic view of the Eucharist as a way of re-presenting Jesus' sacrifice for us. Communion is considered an act of remembrance, a memorial rather than a sacrament by which God conveys his grace; and generally it is observed far less frequently than in the sacramental churches.
- Instead of people coming forward for the Eucharist to receive Christ, they are invited forward to confess publicly their need for Christ and to invite him to forgive their sins and become Lord of their lives.
- Most Baptist churches do not recite the Lord's Prayer during worship, since it was regarded by early Baptist reformers as something that smacked of Catholicism.
- Baptist churches typically do not observe Ash Wednesday, Lent, or Advent, though some churches have begun to explore these ancient holy days and seasons.

Leader Extra
Basic Beliefs and Practices

In spite of the diversity among Baptists, they do share some basic beliefs and practices. Baptists begin with the idea of a believers' church—a church composed of those who have made a confession of faith in Christ. All church members must testify to a work of grace, with baptism viewed as its outward sign. Baptism, therefore, follows confession of faith. Although the practice of affusion—pouring water over the believer three times, in the name of the Father, Son, and Holy Spirit—was followed initially, Baptists began practicing baptism by immersion by 1641; and it has remained the normative mode to this day.

Baptists have a congregational church government, in which clergy and laity work together in the governance of the church. Two types of church officer are recognized: pastors and deacons. Congregational autonomy is highly valued and protected. Individual churches do associate with other churches that are like-minded, however, in order to pursue common goals; these associations are called conventions.

In general, Baptists hold to the essentials of the faith as described in both the Apostles' Creed and the Nicene Creed, though they do not make use of those creeds. Instead they have faith statements that are generally agreed upon by those who associate with a given convention. For Southern Baptists, this statement is called "The Baptist Faith and Message." There is much in this statement that other Protestants would agree with and a few things they might disagree with. Generally, these disagreements spring from differing views of the Bible. Most Protestants look to the Bible as the primary authority for faith and practice, but there is a tendency among Southern Baptists to maintain a more conservative and literal interpretation of Scripture. This is why Southern Baptists officially do not allow women in the pastorate, though American Baptists have embraced the ordination of female clergy.

Three beliefs central to Baptists include the inspiration, infallibility, and preservation of Scripture; the importance of one's personal relationship with God; and salvation by grace through faith alone.

Group Discussion

Note: More questions are provided than you may have time for. Select those you would like your group to discuss.

1. Who were the Puritans, and what kind of reform did they seek to bring to the Church of England?
2. Who were the Pilgrims, and how did they respond to their dissatisfaction with the Church of England?
3. The first Baptists came from what tradition? Why were they considered to be radical reformers? How were they treated?
4. What beliefs and practices of the Church of England did the Baptists reject or discard and why? What was their primary criterion for determining church practice? (See Leader Extra: Distinctive Differences.)
5. Why are religious freedom and congregational autonomy so highly valued among Baptists? How is this reflected in the way Baptist churches are governed?
6. Why are there many different varieties of Baptists? What are some of the differences and similarities among these groups? What is the purpose of conventions among Baptist groups?
7. How are Baptists similar to mainline churches in their beliefs? (See Leader Extra: Basic Beliefs and Practices.)
8. Generally speaking, how do Baptists view the Scriptures? How does their approach to interpreting Scripture tend to differ from that of other Protestant churches?
9. What are three core beliefs or emphases all Baptists hold in common?
10. What three qualities demonstrated by Baptists would all Christians do well to emulate? How are these qualities evident in your church?
11. What have you learned from our study of Baptists that will help to deepen your own faith and experience of God?

Group Activity

Ask participants to complete this sentence: The most-important thing a believer does is . . . Write the responses on a chalkboard or large sheet of paper, making tally marks beside responses that are given more than once. How often was evangelism (sharing one's faith; witnessing) mentioned? On a scale of 1–10, with 10 being most effective, how would you rate your church in the area of evangelism? How would you rate yourself? Discuss effective ways we can share the gospel with others—as individuals and as the church (or as groups within the church).

Wrapping Up

Taking It Home

Briefly review the Taking It Home application exercises included on the Participant Handout. Encourage participants to complete the activities during the coming week, reminding them that they will not be asked to share any details with the group. The exercises are intended for their private use and are designed to help them get the most out of this study that they possibly can.

Invite those participants who have purchased copies of the participant's book to read Chapter 6 this week as a follow-up to this group session. (Those reading chapters in advance of the group sessions will read Chapter 7 this week.)

Notable Quote

"Baptists emphasize making a decision for Christ in a very simple salvation message. . . . Somewhere along the way it's important for you to say, 'I'm choosing to follow Christ.' . . . Sometimes we in the mainline churches have forgotten that. We have thought that if people just come to church, they'll get it by osmosis."

—Adam Hamilton

Closing Prayer

Dear God, thank you for the witness of the Baptist faith tradition, which reminds us of the beautiful simplicity of the gospel message and of your personal, intimate love for each one of us. Thank you for loving us so much that you sent your only Son, Jesus, to walk among us, show us your heart, and save us from sin and death by dying on the cross and then, three days later, rising again. We acknowledge that we all have sinned and gone astray and that we desperately need a Savior. We need Jesus, who gives us hope and peace and abundant life—both now and for all eternity. May we draw ever closer to him by faithfully reading and studying your Word. May it always be a lamp to our feet and a light to our path. In Jesus' name we pray. Amen.

Week 6: Baptists
Participant Handout

For God so loved the world that he gave his only Son, so that everyone who believes in him may not perish but may have eternal life. (John 3:16)

Key Insights

1. In the 1600s, the Puritans sought to purge the church of its Catholic elements; to restore it to what they believed was its New Testament character; and to purify the church and its members, challenging them to lead a holy life.
2. The more-radical Puritans left the church; among these were the Pilgrims. Another group of Puritans who called for more-radical reform and eventually left the church were the Baptists.
3. Baptists believed that only those practices explicitly described in the New Testament were to be made normative for the church. Consequently, they reasoned that infant baptism should be eliminated. Baptists were first called Anapedopbaptist (those against the baptism of infants).
4. John Smyth was the first Baptist pastor on record. He established his church in 1609.
5. Baptists rejected anything in church practice that appeared "Catholic," such as the liturgical elements of worship, the formal acts of worship, and the vestments or dress of the clergy.
6. Baptists were persecuted by both the Puritans and the Church of England. Consequently, they have traditionally had a strong appreciation for the separation of church and state.
7. There are many different varieties of Baptists. Although the autonomy of a given Baptist church is protected, Baptist churches associate with other churches that are like-minded in conventions.

8. Three core beliefs or emphases of all Baptists: 1) The inspiration, infallibility, and preservation of Scripture; 2) The importance of one's personal relationship with God; 3) Salvation by grace through faith alone.
9. Baptists demonstrate three qualities all Christians can learn from: 1) A love of God's Word and Bible study; 2) An emphasis on missions and evangelism; 3) The simple salvation message.

Taking It Home

This week you will read and pray through the longest psalm in the Bible, Psalm 119. Its focus is on pursuing God's Word and commands—an important theme to Baptists and to all Christians.

- Read Psalm 119:1-40 aloud as a prayer. What does it mean to seek God with all your heart and to walk in God's ways? How does God's Word help you in this? What other benefits does reading and studying God's Word provide?
- Read Psalm 119:41-88 aloud as a prayer. Note the psalmist's steadfastness even during times of trouble and affliction. How has God's Word been a source of comfort, strength, and hope to you in difficult times? Offer a prayer of gratitude.
- Read Psalm 119:89-144. Choose a portion of these verses and read them aloud as a prayer. Invite God to guide you in the truth and to direct your path.
- Read Psalm 119:145-176. Choose a portion of these verses and read them aloud as a prayer. Which of these verses speaks most clearly to you as you pray?

PENTECOSTALISM:
THE POWER OF THE SPIRIT

Main Idea: Pentecostalism reminds us that we need to invite the Holy Spirit to be at work in our lives.

Getting Started

Session Goals
This session is intended to help participants...
- become familiar with the beginnings of the Pentecostal tradition;
- understand some of the beliefs and practices of Pentecostalism;
- affirm the importance and power of the Holy Spirit;
- recognize our need to invite the Holy Spirit to be at work in our lives.

Opening Prayer
Dear God, we come together today to learn about another branch of the Christian family tree, Pentecostalism. We ask you to keep us mindful that our aim is not to critique the Pentecostal faith tradition but to learn from it so that our own faith might be enriched. Help us through our study and discussion to become more authentic and effective disciples of your Son, Jesus Christ. We affirm that all who call upon his name are members of one body, one faith. May we be united in spirit, in love, and in service so that your kingdom work may be accomplished in our world. In Jesus' name we pray. Amen.

Biblical Foundation

> *I will pour out my Spirit on all flesh.*
> *(Joel 2:28)*

> *You will receive power when the Holy Spirit has come upon you; and you will be my witnesses in Jerusalem, in all Judea and Samaria, and to the ends of the earth. (Acts 1:8)*

> *When the day of Pentecost had come, they were all together in one place. And suddenly from heaven there came a sound like the rush of a violent wind, and it filled the entire house where they were sitting. Divided tongues, as of fire, appeared among them, and a tongue rested on each of them. All of them were filled with the Holy Spirit and began to speak in other languages, as the Spirit gave them ability. (Acts 2:1-4)*

Opening Activity

Ask: What are some of the roles of the Holy Spirit? What are some ways the Spirit works in our lives—individually and corporately (as the church)? List the responses on a chalkboard or large sheet of paper. Discuss: What are some specific ways we can open ourselves to the work of the Holy Spirit?

Learning Together

Video Presentation

Play the video segment for Week 7, *Pentecostalism.*
Running Time: 16:28 minutes

Key Insights

1. Pentecostalism takes its name from the Jewish festival of Pentecost; it was at this festival around AD 30 that the Holy Spirit descended on the first Christians, and the church was born. Pentecostals are known for energetic and passion-filled worship and an emphasis on supernatural experiences of the Holy Spirit.

2. Although the official beginning of Pentecostalism is usually set at 1901, its roots reach back another 200 years through John Wesley and the Methodist Church, which was known for its spiritual passion and emphasis on the work of the Holy Spirit.

3. In nineteenth-century America, a number of groups broke away from the Methodist movement to form their own churches. They included the Nazarenes and their predecessors, the Church of God (Anderson, Indiana); the Adventists; the Salvation Army; the Wesleyan Church; and others. These groups tended to be more conservative theologically than the Methodists, and they placed a greater emphasis on holiness or sanctification. Pentecostalism was born out of this holiness movement in 1901 at Bethel Bible College in Topeka, Kansas. For more details, see Leader Extra: The Official Beginning of Pentecostalism.

4. The baptism or infilling of the Holy Spirit, characterized by speaking in an unknown tongue (or in a language one has not previously known), is what defines Pentecostals. Those in non-Pentecostal denominations who have had this experience are typically called "Charismatics," from the Greek word used in the New Testament for spiritual gifts (*charismata*).

5. Four major emphases of Pentecostalism:

   1) *The baptism or infilling of the Holy Spirit.* Pentecostals believe that after the Spirit comes upon us when we commit our lives to Christ, there is a subsequent experience (called a "second work of grace") at which time the Holy Spirit completely immerses believers, filling them with power. The evidence of the baptism of the Holy Spirit is speaking in an unknown tongue.

   2) *Having a personal relationship with Jesus Christ.* Pentecostals place a strong emphasis on the emotional dimensions of one's relationship with Jesus Christ.

   3) *The second coming of Jesus Christ.* Pentecostals recall the words of Joel 2:28, which says, "I will pour out my Spirit on all flesh." The experience that Charles Fox Parham (founder

of Bethel Bible College in Topeka, Kansas) and others had of being baptized by the Holy Spirit was seen as a direct fulfillment of this passage from Joel and a sure sign that the Second Coming was about to take place. This belief has been a hallmark of Pentecostal preaching ever since. Most Pentecostal pastors will not predict dates for the Lord's return, but for many years it was taught that the Lord would return before 1988—forty years after the reconstitution of the nation of Israel in 1948.

4) *Modern-day miracles and healing.* Jesus himself promised we would see miracles happen (Mark 16:17; Luke 21:11, 25). The Book of James (5:14) assures us that if any are sick and call for the elders of the church and are anointed with oil, the prayer of faith will raise them up. There is a greater sense of expectation within Pentecostal churches that God is in the "miracle-working business."

6. Three things all Christians can learn from Pentecostalism:

1) We need to live daily in the power of the Holy Spirit. The gift of the Holy Spirit is like anything else God offers us: God gives us the gift, but it is up to us to accept it by inviting the Spirit to work in us.

2) We need to identify and use our spiritual gifts.

3) We need to reclaim the healing power of the Holy Spirit.

Leader Extra

The Official Beginning of Pentecostalism

Charles Fox Parham, who had a Methodist background, was teaching at Bethel Bible College in Topeka, Kansas. Parham's study of the Book of Acts led him to wonder if the works of the Holy Spirit recorded there could not still happen in the church. He came to believe that what he called "baptism in the Holy Spirit" was separate from the believer's receipt of the Holy Spirit at salvation.

Parham felt that such an experience—an immersion in the Holy Spirit—would be demonstrated first by speaking in tongues, whereby the Holy Spirit enabled Christians to speak in a language they had not previously known or to speak in a completely unintelligible language.

Parham began to invite his students to receive this manifestation of the Holy Spirit, and it was in 1901 that a woman named Agnes Ozman had an experience such as Parham had described and began to speak in an unintelligible language.

Several years later Parham and a man named William J. Seymour were preaching at a revival in an old abandoned Methodist church in Los Angeles, and the Holy Spirit fell upon the people there. From there the Pentecostal fire spread across the country and throughout the world.

Group Discussion

Note: More questions are provided than you may have time for. Select those you would like your group to discuss.

1. From where does Pentecostalism take its name, and why is this significant?
2. Discuss how the Pentecostal faith tradition was born over a period of several hundred years:
   - How are the roots of Pentecostalism connected to Methodism?
   - What was the holiness movement in nineteenth-century America? What churches were formed as a result of this movement? What did they have in common?
   - When, where, and how did Pentecostalism officially begin? Who was Charles Fox Parham, and what role did he play?
3. Read Matthew 3:11. What did John the Baptist say about the Holy Spirit? What do Pentecostals believe happens to believers when they commit their lives to Christ? What is the "second work of grace" that they believe follows the salvation experience?
4. How might a Pentecostal describe or define the baptism or infilling of the Holy Spirit? Why do they believe this experience is important? What does it produce in the believer's life?
5. Why do you think Pentecostals place a strong emphasis on the emotional dimensions of one's relationship with Jesus Christ? Do

you know of any ways this emphasis on the emotions or feelings is evidenced in Pentecostal worship?

6. Read Joel 2:28. What do Pentecostals believe about this passage? Why do they believe that the second coming of Christ is imminent—within our lifetimes?

7. What is the Pentecostal view on miracles and healing? Why do you think there is a greater sense of expectation within Pentecostal churches that God is in the "miracle-working business"? Why do you think many Christians are often reluctant to ask God to do great things—as individuals and as the church?

8. Do you believe most Christians take seriously the role of the Holy Spirit in their lives? Why or why not?

9. How can we live in the power and direction of the Holy Spirit? Why is it important *daily* to invite the Holy Spirit to be at work in us?

10. Read 1 Corinthians 12:7-11, 28. What are the spiritual gifts Paul names in these verses? What gift does he mention in Ephesians 4:11? Read 1 Peter 4:10-11. What gifts do you have (or think you may have), and how are you using them?

11. What have you learned from our study of Pentecostalism that will help to deepen your own faith and experience of God?

Group Activity

Have participants form groups of two (other than spouses) and take turns sharing ways they have experienced the Holy Spirit at work in their lives. (How have they experienced the Holy Spirit as Comforter, Counselor, Guide, and so forth?)

Wrapping Up

Taking It Home

Briefly review the Taking It Home application exercises included on the Participant Handout. Encourage participants to complete the activities during the coming week, reminding them that they will not be asked to share any details with the group. The exercises are intended for their private use and are designed to help them get the most out of this study that they possibly can.

Invite those participants who have purchased copies of the participant's book to read Chapter 7 this week as a follow-up to this group session. (Those reading chapters in advance of the group sessions will have already read the chapter.)

Notable Quote

"We have to invite the Spirit to work, but many times we do what my children used to do when they were little . . . they would say, 'No, I can do it myself.' . . . We try to live the Christian life on our own without inviting the power of the Holy Spirit."

—*Adam Hamilton*

Closing Prayer

Dear God, thank you for the witness of the Pentecostal faith tradition, which reminds us of the power and presence of your Holy Spirit. Help us to be more intentional about inviting your Spirit to be at work in our lives each and every day; we know that doing this will result in our experiencing and being more aware of the Spirit's guidance, power, and work in our lives. So we ask you now, Holy Spirit, to come and fill us anew. Guide us. Use us. Empower us. Lead us. Grant us your gifts that we might be useful to you in serving others. In Jesus' name we pray. Amen.

Week 7: Pentecostalism
Participant Handout

I will pour out my Spirit on all flesh.
(Joel 2:28)

Key Insights

1. Pentecostalism takes its name from the Jewish festival of Pentecost; it was at this festival around AD 30 that the Holy Spirit descended on the first Christians, and the church was born. Pentecostals are known for energetic and passion-filled worship and an emphasis on supernatural experiences of the Holy Spirit.

2. Although the official beginning of Pentecostalism is usually set at 1901, its roots reach back another 200 years through John Wesley and the Methodist Church, which was known for its spiritual passion and emphasis on the work of the Holy Spirit.

3. In nineteenth-century America, a number of groups broke away from the Methodist movement to form their own churches. They included the Nazarenes and their predecessors, the Church of God (Anderson, Indiana); the Adventists; the Salvation Army; the Wesleyan Church; and others. These groups tended to be more conservative theologically than the Methodists, and they placed a greater emphasis on holiness or sanctification. Pentecostalism was born out of this holiness movement in 1901 at Bethel Bible College in Topeka, Kansas.

4. The baptism or infilling of the Holy Spirit, characterized by speaking in an unknown tongue (or in a language one has not previously known), is what defines Pentecostals. Those in non-Pentecostal denominations who have had this experience are typically called "Charismatics," from the Greek word used in the New Testament for spiritual gifts (*charismata*).

5. Four major emphases of Pentecostalism:
   1) *The baptism of the Holy Spirit.* Pentecostals believe that after the

Spirit comes upon us when we commit our lives to Christ, there is a subsequent experience (called a "second work of grace") at which time the Holy Spirit completely immerses believers, filling them with power. The evidence of this experience is speaking in an unknown tongue (or in a language one has not previously known).

2) *Having a personal relationship with Jesus Christ.* Pentecostals place a strong emphasis on the emotional dimensions of one's relationship with Jesus Christ.

3) *The second coming of Jesus Christ.* Pentecostals recall the words of Joel 2:28, which says, "I will pour out my Spirit on all flesh." The experience that Parham and others had of being baptized by the Holy Spirit was seen as a direct fulfillment of this passage and a sure sign that the Second Coming was about to take place. This belief has been a hallmark of Pentecostal preaching ever since.

4) *Modern-day miracles and healing.* Jesus himself promised we would see miracles happen (Mark 16:17; Luke 21:11, 25). The Book of James (5:14) assures us that if any are sick and call for the elders of the church and are anointed with oil, the prayer of faith will raise them up. There is a greater sense of expectation within Pentecostal churches that God is in the "miracle-working business."

6. Three things all Christians can learn from Pentecostalism:

1) We need to live daily in the power of the Holy Spirit. The gift of the Holy Spirit is like anything else God offers us: God gives us the gift, but it is up to us to accept it by inviting the Spirit to work in us.

2) We need to identify and use our spiritual gifts.

3) We need to reclaim the healing power of the Holy Spirit.

Taking It Home

• Read Matthew 3:11; Mark 13:9-11; Luke 11:13. What do these verses teach us about the Holy Spirit? Invite the Holy Spirit to lead, guide, and speak through you.

- Read John 14:15-21, 25-27. What does it mean to call the Spirit our "Counselor" or "Advocate"? Now read John 16:5-15. What does Jesus say the Holy Spirit will do? Invite the Holy Spirit to do for you what Jesus promises.
- Read Acts 1:1-8. What will the Holy Spirit do for believers? Now read Acts 2:1-21. What happened as the Holy Spirit came upon the disciples? What was the purpose of this gift, and how did it work? How is this different than most modern Pentecostal expressions of tongues? Pray for the outpouring of the Spirit upon your life.
- The Holy Spirit gives different gifts to each believer to help build up the Christian community. Read 1 Corinthians 12:1-31. What are the gifts Paul mentions? What is their purpose? How does Paul correct those who thought some gifts were more important than others? Invite the Holy Spirit to help you discover and use the gifts you have been given.
- Read Romans 8:1-17. What does the Spirit do in and through us? Paul suggests that it is not the exotic gifts of the Spirit that are the measure of one's spiritual life but certain fruit that the Holy Spirit produces in us. Read Galatians 5:16-26, focusing on verses 22-23. Invite the Holy Spirit to produce this fruit in you.

METHODISM: PEOPLE OF THE EXTREME CENTER

Main Idea: The Methodist faith tradition shows us the importance of embracing seeming contradictions and finding balance in the life of faith.

Getting Started

Session Goals

This session is intended to help participants...

- learn about John Wesley and the beginnings of Methodism;
- become familiar with some of the beliefs and practices of Methodists;
- understand why Methodists are a people of the "extreme center";
- recognize how Methodism is a blending of both Anglican and Puritan traditions;
- recognize the interconnectedness and beauty of the Christian family tree.

Opening Prayer

Dear God, we come together today to learn about another branch of the Christian family tree, Methodism. We ask you to keep us mindful that our aim is not to critique the Methodist faith tradition but to learn from it so that our own faith might be enriched. Help us through our study and discussion to become more authentic and effective disciples of your Son, Jesus Christ. We affirm that all who call upon his name are members of one body, one faith. May we be united in spirit, in love, and in service so that your kingdom work may be accomplished in our world. In Jesus' name we pray. Amen.

Biblical Foundation

When he left there, he met Jehonadab son of Rechab coming to meet him; he greeted him, and said to him, "Is your heart as true to mine as mine is to yours?" Jehonadab answered, "It is." Jehu said, "If it is, give me your hand." (2 Kings 10:15)

When the Pharisees heard that he had silenced the Sadducees, they gathered together, and one of them, a lawyer, asked him a question to test him. "Teacher, which commandment in the law is the greatest?" He said to him, "'You shall love the Lord your God with all your heart, and with all your soul, and with all your mind.' This is the greatest and first commandment." (Matthew 22:34-38)

Opening Activity

Say: Bishop Scott Jones has said that Methodists are people of the "extreme center." Discuss: What do you think he means by this? Do you believe that truth often is found most fully not on the extremes, but in the center? Why or why not? In what ways is maintaining balance important to the life of faith?

Learning Together

Video Presentation

Play the video segment for Week 8, *Methodism*.
Running Time: 16:46 minutes

Key Insights

1. In the early eighteenth century, many in England were tired of the religious conflict and warfare that had been taking place for

almost two hundred years. John Wesley, founder of the Methodist movement, was among them. Wesley wanted to build bridges instead of walls. This became part of the spirit of Methodism.

2. Wesley's desire was to be wholly committed to Christ—to be Christian in practice as well as in name. He devoted his entire life to calling people to a radical commitment to Jesus Christ. For more information on Wesley, see Leader Extra: About John Wesley.

3. In his early years, Wesley knew God with his intellect but not with his heart, though he longed to experience an assurance of his salvation. Then one evening while attending the meeting of a religious society, he felt his heart "strangely warmed." From that moment he had an assurance of his salvation, and his ministry was characterized by new passion and vitality.

4. John Wesley spent the rest of his life proclaiming the goodness of Jesus Christ, often traveling from town to town on horseback. It is said that he traveled 250,000 miles by horseback in his lifetime, preaching the gospel.

5. The Methodists were known for an emphasis not only on the call to conversion but also on what happens after that. Wesley organized people into "societies," which were small groups that met together for preaching, teaching, prayer, and accountability. These gatherings were called Methodist class meetings.

6. Another emphasis of Methodism was loving one's neighbor as oneself, or the social gospel. Wesley brought together the evangelical and social gospels.

7. Methodists are people of the extreme center, which means they hold on to a theological position that embraces conservative and liberal, personal faith and social outreach, intellect and emotions. To this day United Methodists see themselves as people who bring together both a reasonable faith that is intellectually satisfying and a passionate and emotionally compelling faith that touches the heart.

8. John Wesley devoted his life to three passions:
   1) He wanted to change lives. (Wesley invited people to know Jesus Christ and to pour their entire lives into following him.)
   2) He wanted to change the community. (Wesley believed in spreading scriptural holiness across the land and in applying the gospel to every part of life.)
   3) He wanted to reform and revitalize the church of his day.
9. The body of Christ is like a tree. The beauty of the tree is in all its branches, which share the same trunk, Jesus Christ, and the same roots, Judaism. The sap that feeds the leaves is the Holy Spirit, which permeates every branch. We are connected to all our Christian brothers and sisters.

Leader Extra
About John Wesley

John Wesley was born June 17, 1703. He was the fifteenth of nineteen children of Samuel and Susanna Wesley. Wesley's grandfathers had been "Dissenters" (those who were dissatisfied with the official state church and who formed their own churches). Wesley's father was a priest in the Church of England.

John ultimately followed his father's footsteps into the ministry, studying at Christ Church (College), Oxford. There he wrote that his desire was no longer to be a "nominal" Christian but to be a "real" Christian. Following his ordination and a brief stint in the local church, he returned to Oxford, where he tutored and began to meet with a group of students who also longed for a more-rigorous faith. These students met several times a week to study the classics as well as religious works, and they worshiped together and pursued acts of charity in the community. Their methodical approach to the pursuit of holiness earned them the name "Methodist" among their critics. The name stuck.

Wesley was shaped both by the spirit of the Enlightenment and by the Pietist movement that was skeptical of reason, holding these seemingly opposing forces together in tension with each other. This union of reason with the desire for a personal faith would become a defining characteristic of Methodism.

In the early years, Wesley's own faith leaned more toward the intellect. Then, in 1738, Wesley had what he considered to be a profound conversion experience. In words that are among his most famous, he described what happened to him while attending a gathering of a religious society. As he listened to the words of Martin Luther being read—words reflecting upon the teaching of justification by faith—he reported, "I felt my heart strangely warmed. I felt I did trust in Christ, Christ alone for salvation; and an assurance was given me that He had taken away my sins, even mine, and saved me from the law of sin and death."[1] Wesley demonstrated a new passion and religious zeal following this experience.

When Wesley's friend George Whitefield asked him to come and preach in the fields, a practice that Wesley initially viewed as improper and distasteful, he declined. In April of 1739, however, he finally relented. There was no turning back from this form of preaching. Wesley proclaimed that "the world is my parish." He would spend the rest of his life preaching in the open air, and in churches when invited. By the time of Wesley's death, he was a national hero; and his preaching and leadership had changed the course of history.

Leader Extra
Methodist Beliefs and Practices
- Methodists accept the Nicene Creed and Apostles' Creed as containing the core tenets of the Christian faith, and many congregations recite one or the other weekly in their worship services. The officially binding theological statements are not the creeds, but what are called the "Articles of Religion," which are drawn from the Anglican Church's Articles of Religion.
- Methodists are ecumenical and willing to work with and learn from Christians of other denominations.
- Methodists believe in bringing their intellect to their faith.
- Methodists value both passion and experience. This combination

of reason and experience—the intellectual pursuit of God with spiritual fervor and passion—is part of the basic makeup of Methodism. Wesley added experience to the Anglicans' three-legged stool of Scripture, tradition, and reason to create what is referred to as the Wesleyan quadrilateral.

• Methodists place an emphasis on a personal faith, recognizing the importance of the "new birth," the spiritual disciplines, the personal devotional life, the laity in the church, and small-group meetings to study the Scriptures.

• Methodists believe that God's grace is available to and working in all of us and that we are free to accept it or reject it. They accept the idea that God may know in advance what will happen and who will choose God, but they reject the idea that God has foreordained who will inherit eternal life.

• Wesley brought together the high-church tradition of the Anglicans with the low-church simplicity of worship that characterized Puritan churches. Most Methodist services today include elements of worship that are Anglican, though less liturgical, along with elements of the Presbyterian worship that sprang from the Puritan traditions.

• Methodists emphasize both grace and holiness. Methodists recognize that our salvation is purely a gift from God. At the same time, they believe that we are saved from sin in order to do good works. Wesley emphasized a doctrine called sanctification (Christian perfection or holiness), which means to have one's heart so transformed by the power of the Holy Spirit that one manifests perfect love for God and neighbor. Wesley believed it was possible to be wholly sanctified in this life and that, by the pursuit of God and the yielding of one's life to the work of the Holy Spirit, anyone might receive from God this gift of sanctification.

Group Discussion

Note: More questions are provided than you may have time for. Select those you would like your group to discuss.

1. What was the religious climate in England in the early eighteenth century?

2. Who was John Wesley, and what was his personal spiritual desire? How did this desire shape his life and ministry? (See Leader Extra: About John Wesley.)

3. What is the significance of Christ Church (College), Oxford, to Methodism? How did Methodists get their name? (See Leader Extra: About John Wesley.)

4. What was Wesley's experience of God in his early years? What was his struggle? When and how did he receive an assurance of his salvation, and what effect did this have on his ministry?

5. When asked why people came to hear him preach, Wesley said, "I set myself on fire and people come to watch me burn." What does this remark suggest to you about Wesley's preaching?

6. How was Wesley an advocate of political and social issues in his day? What two "gospels" did he successfully unite?

7. How are we to live as followers of Jesus Christ if we truly love our neighbors as ourselves? How can we find the right balance between the inner experience and the outward expression of our faith?

8. In what ways are United Methodists people of the "extreme center"?

9. What three passions did Wesley pursue all his life? Do you believe these are still appropriate passions or objectives for the church today? Why or why not?

10. What have you learned from our study of Methodism that will help to deepen your own faith and experience of God?

Concluding Questions

1. Adam Hamilton suggests that the body of Christ can be compared to a tree with many branches, all sharing the same trunk, roots, and sap. What would happen if we tried to cut off all the other branches of the tree, leaving only our own branch? What do the trunk, roots, and sap represent?

2. Adam Hamilton suggests that when we look at the church as a tree, we should be moved to say, "How beautiful is the body of Christ! How grateful we are for all its branches!" How does looking at the church as a tree affect your attitude toward other denominations and faith traditions? How has this study impacted your understanding of and/or appreciation for other branches of the Christian family tree?

3. How can we help to build bridges instead of walls in the body of Christ? What can your church do to foster a spirit of ecumenicalism in your community? What opportunities exist for cooperative ministry, service, or worship?

Group Activity
List the following three passions of John Wesley on a chalkboard or large sheet of paper:

1) A passion for changing lives
2) A passion for changing the community
3) A passion for reforming and revitalizing the church

Discuss ways that your church might strategically pursue each of these goals...

- as a church (begin with any current ministries, activities, and events of your church that relate to each of these goals);
- as individuals;
- and as a cooperative effort of various denominations or faith groups within your community.

Wrapping Up

Taking It Home
Briefly review the Taking It Home application exercises included on the Participant Handout. Encourage participants to complete the

activities during the coming week, reminding them that they will not be asked to share any details with the group. The exercises are intended for their private use and are designed to help them get the most out of this study that they possibly can.

Invite those participants who have purchased copies of the participant's book to read Chapter 8 this week as a follow-up to this group session. (Those reading chapters in advance of the group sessions will have already read the chapter.)

Notable Quote

"We are at our best when we are listening to other people and learning from them . . . and asking the question, What does it mean to be a follower of Jesus Christ here and now in this place?"

—Adam Hamilton

Closing Prayer

Almighty God, how grateful we are for the Methodist tradition, which encourages us to have a faith that is both intellectually sound and emotionally passionate. Help us to love you with everything that is within us—to be deeply devoted to you. Help us to claim the social gospel—to have the courage to speak out and to raise questions in our society, even if we do not have all the answers. As we conclude our study, we offer our gratitude for the gift of the church. We acknowledge that each branch has a beauty all its own. Forgive us for secretly believing we are your favorites. Help us to love our Christian brothers and sisters and to continue learning from them. May we always see them as your beloved children. In Jesus' name. Amen.

1. From *The Works of John Wesley,* edited by Albert C. Outler (Abingdon Press, 1988); Vol. 18; entry for May 24, 1738.

Week 8: Methodism
Participant Handout

"'You shall love the Lord your God with all your heart, and with all your soul, and with all your mind.' This is the greatest and first commandment." *(Matthew 22:37-38)*

Key Insights

1. John Wesley, founder of the Methodist movement, was among those who were tired of the religious conflict and warfare that had been taking place in England for almost two hundred years. Wesley wanted to build bridges instead of walls. This became part of the spirit of Methodism.

2. Wesley's desire was to be wholly committed to Christ. He devoted his life to calling people to a radical commitment to Jesus Christ.

3. In his early years, Wesley knew God with his intellect but not with his heart. Then one evening while attending the gathering of a religious society, he felt his heart "strangely warmed." From that moment he had an assurance of his salvation, and his ministry was characterized by new passion and vitality.

4. John Wesley spent the rest of his life proclaiming the goodness of Christ, traveling from town to town on horseback. It is said he traveled 250,000 miles by horseback in his lifetime, preaching the gospel.

5. The Methodists were known for an emphasis not only on the call to conversion but also on what happens after that. Wesley organized people into "societies"—small groups that met for preaching, teaching, prayer, and accountability. These gatherings were called Methodist class meetings.

6. Another emphasis of Methodism was loving one's neighbor as oneself, or the social gospel. Wesley brought together the evangelical and social gospels.

7. Methodists are people of the extreme center; they hold on to

a theological position that embraces conservative and liberal, personal faith and social outreach, intellect and emotions. To this day United Methodists see themselves as people who bring together both a reasonable faith that is intellectually satisfying and an emotionally compelling faith that touches the heart.

8. John Wesley devoted his life to three passions:
   1) He wanted to change lives. (Wesley invited people to know Jesus Christ and to pour their entire lives into following him.)
   2) He wanted to change the community. (Wesley believed in spreading scriptural holiness across the land and in applying the gospel to every part of life.)
   3) He wanted to reform and revitalize the church of his day.

9. The body of Christ is like a tree. The beauty of the tree is in all its branches, which share the same trunk, Jesus Christ, and the same roots, Judaism. The sap that feeds the leaves is the Holy Spirit, which permeates every branch. We are connected to all our Christian brothers and sisters.

Taking It Home

Jesus' Sermon on the Mount was considered by John Wesley to be the "spirit and essence of religion." This week you will be reading and meditating on the Sermon on the Mount.

- Read Matthew 5:1-12—the Beatitudes. Invite God to help you to be what the Beatitudes commend. Read Matthew 5:13-16. What did Jesus mean when he called his disciples salt? What did he mean when he said we are to be light and a lamp? Invite God to make you salt and light.
- Read Matthew 5:17-20. Moses called for external obedience, but Jesus called people to holiness of heart. Use each section of the following verses as an opportunity to approach God in prayer. Read Matthew 5:21-26, 27-30, 31-32, 33-37, 38-42, 43-48. Which verses speak most clearly to you?
- Read Matthew 6:1-4, 5-15, 16-18. Use these verses as a guide for

a time of prayer. Are you ever tempted to do your "acts of right-eousness" so that others may see you?

- Read Matthew 6:19-21. How do these verses speak to you? Read Matthew 6:22-34. What does it mean to seek first God's kingdom? Read Matthew 7:1-6. How do you tend to judge others or look for the speck in your neighbor's eye while ignoring the log in your own eye? Ask for God's forgiveness and God's help in leaving behind this practice. Read Matthew 7:7-12, which includes the Golden Rule.

- Read Matthew 7:13-14. What does it mean to say that the way to heaven is narrow as opposed to broad? Read Matthew 7:15-23. What is disturbing about these verses? Pray that God will help produce good fruit in your life. Read Matthew 7:24-29. Are you a wise or foolish builder? Invite God to help you put Jesus' words into practice.